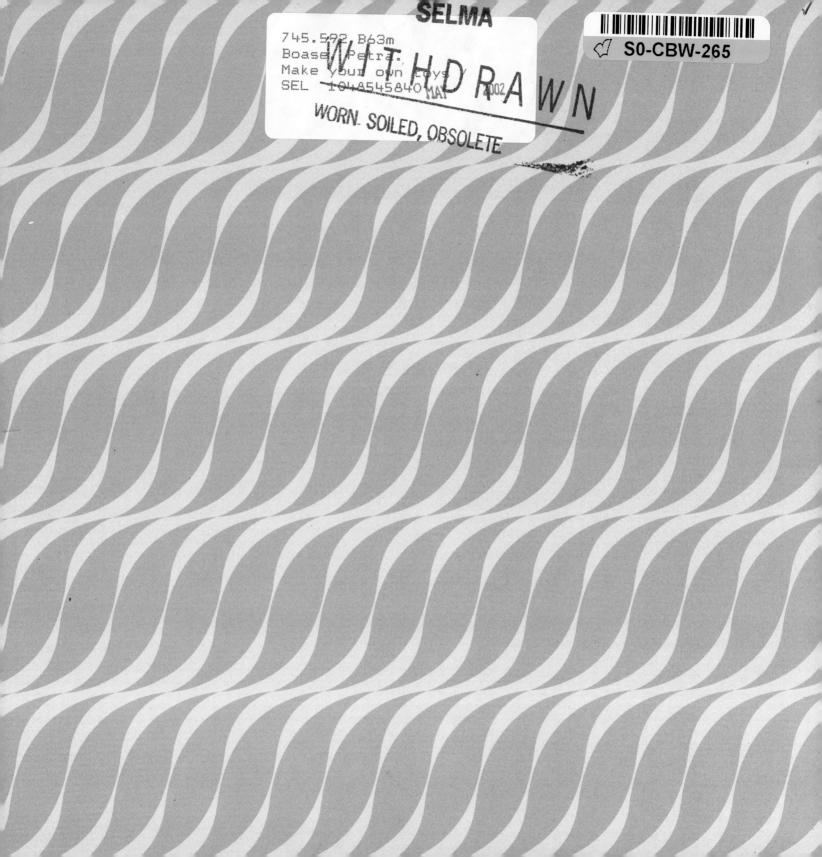

Make Your Own Toys

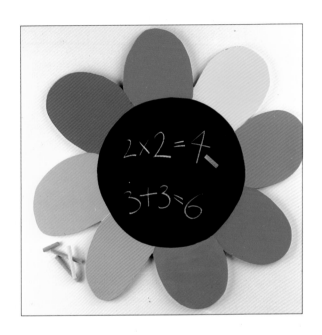

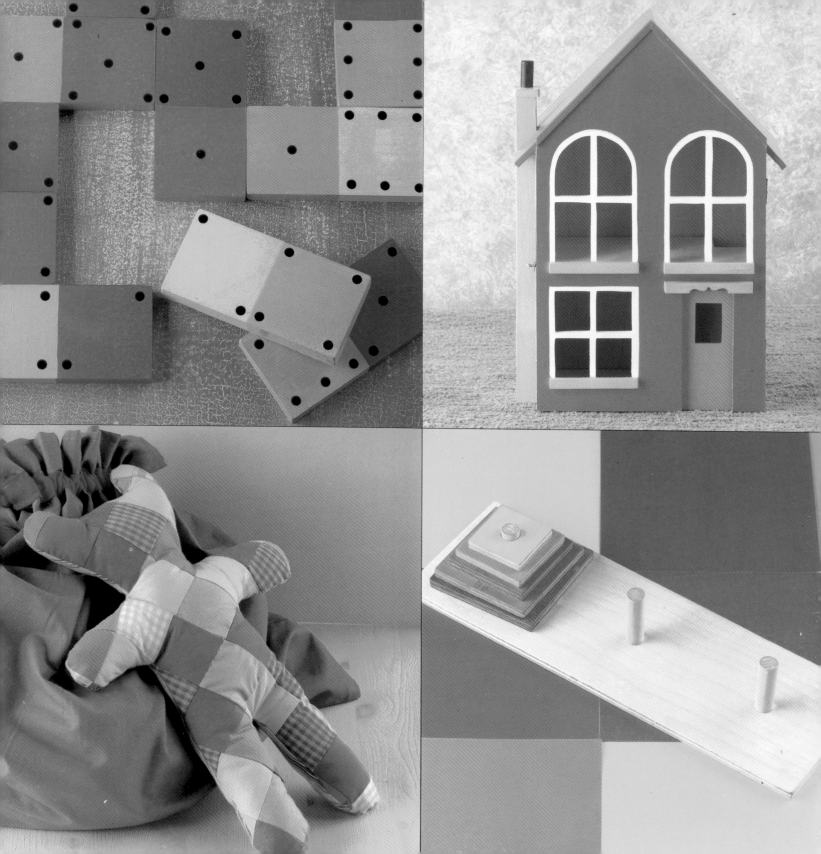

Make Your Own Toys

simple projects for making beautiful and lasting gifts for your babies and children

Petra Boase
Photography by James Duncan

southwater

PUBLISHER'S NOTE

*Crafts and hobbies are great fun to learn and can fill hours of
rewarding leisure time, but some points should be remembered for
safety and care of the environment.*

*• Always choose non-toxic materials wherever possible, for example,
paint, glue and varnish. Where these are not suitable
use materials in a well-ventilated area and always follow
manufacturer's instructions.*

*• Craft knives, drills and all sharp tools should be handled with care.
When sawing or drilling wood, make sure that the wood cannot slip.*

*• Protect surfaces with a cutting mat when using cutting tools and
with newspaper when using paint and glue.*

SOME USEFUL TERMS

UK	US
card	cardboard
PVA glue	white glue
emulsion paint	latex paint
poppers	snap fasteners
MDF	fiberboard
wool	yarn
tack	baste

This edition is published by Southwater

Southwater is an imprint of
Anness Publishing Limited
Hermes House
88–89 Blackfriars Road
London SE1 8HA
tel. 020 7401 2077
fax 020 7633 9499

Distributed in the UK by
The Manning Partnership
251–253 London Road East
Batheaston
Bath BA1 7RL
tel. 01225 852 727
fax 01225 852 852

Distributed in the USA by
Anness Publishing Inc.
27 West 20th Street
Suite 504
New York
NY 10011
fax 212 807 6813

Distributed in Australia by
Sandstone Publishing
Unit 1
360 Norton Street
Leichhardt
New South Wales 2040
tel. 02 9560 7888
fax 02 9560 7488

1 3 5 7 9 10 8 6 4 2

Publisher: Joanna Lorenz
Project Editors: Judith Simons and Joanna Bentley
Designer: Lilian Lindblom
Photography: James Duncan
Stylist: Petra Boase
Illustrator: Lucinda Ganderton

The author and publishers wish to thank David and Jill Hancock for
their contribution to this book

Previously published as *Step-by-step: 50 Toys to Make*

CONTENTS

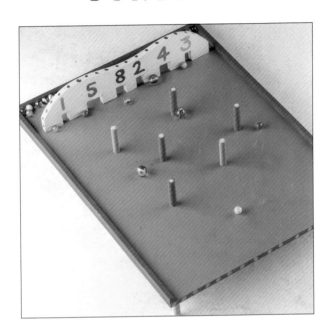

INTRODUCTION

Toys are a very important part of a child's growing years. Through playing with toys so much is learnt and enjoyed - colour, touch and sound are only a few of the pleasures.

The exciting range of projects in this book incorporates all kinds of materials and techniques. Many of them enable you to save odds and ends from around the home and recycle them. It is a useful idea to keep a cardboard box near the kitchen so you can store bottles, newspapers, etc. until you are ready to use them.

When you are making the toys it is very important to focus on the finishing touches. For example, when gluing materials together make sure they are secure after the glue has dried. If you are working with wood, smooth all the surfaces and corners thoroughly with sandpaper before painting, to avoid splinters.

The most important thing is to have fun making the projects. I hope the children you are making the toys for appreciate your creativity. Good luck!

Materials

These are some of the materials used in this book

Bottles

Only use plastic bottles for the projects. Save bottle tops for decoration. However, they are not suitable for decorating babies' toys.

Card (cardboard) and paper

Card comes in a range of thicknesses. It sometimes needs to be cut with a craft knife rather than scissors. Newspaper is the core material used for papier-mâché.

Decorations

These are incredibly wide-ranging and the only curb on your imagination is making absolutely sure that the decoration you have chosen for a toy is suitable for the age of the child you are making it for. All decorations should be very firmly attached. Choose from buttons (look in charity shops for unusual examples), furnishing fringing, coloured pipe-cleaners, and pretty ribbons, including ribbon roses, sticky shapes, even shoelaces.

Fabrics

The choice of colours, patterns and textures is as wide as you could wish for. You may prefer to choose natural materials, such as cotton and linen. Felt is beautifully soft and has the added advantage of being easy to cut without fraying. It is also available with an adhesive backing for covering objects.

Fasteners

Paper fasteners can be used to join two pieces of card (cardboard) or paper together, while still allowing them to move. Poppers (snap fasteners) or press studs, are used for fastening fabric. Velcro is a quick and easy fastener for fabric.

Glues and tapes

Double-sided tape can be used instead of glue to stick paper or card (cardboard). Electrical tape is very strong and can be used to fasten heavy materials. It can also be used for decoration and it comes in a wide range of primary colours. Masking tape is very useful for reinforcing card (cardboard) shapes and for marking out areas before painting. PVA (white) glue is a water-based, non-toxic glue and ideal for sticking wood or paper. It can also be diluted with water and used in papier-mâché or as a quick and easy varnish.

Paints

Water-based paints are non-toxic and ideal for babies' and children's toys. Choose from either poster, acrylic or emulsion (latex) paints. Enamel paints are oil-based paints which will adhere to metal, wood or plastic. Spray paints are mostly toxic when wet, so use them outdoors or in a well-ventilated room and always wear a mask.

Polymer clay

This is a modelling medium that is available in a range of colours. Always follow the manufacturer's instructions, as products do vary.

Safety pin

Use this to help thread ribbon or cord through a fabric tube.

Screw eyes

These are screwed into the back of a piece of wood (for example, a picture frame) and cord can be attached to them for hanging.

Stuffing

This is used to fill toys and shapes made from fabric.

Ties

Cord is stronger than either string or ribbon and can be threaded through a drawstring bag to pull it shut. Rope is stronger still, although nylon rope does tend to unravel at the ends unless you seal them by burning (see Techniques).

Threads

Embroidery threads are used in hand sewing to make colourful, detailed stitches. For ordinary hand or machine sewing choose either cotton or rayon thread.

Wood

Balsa wood is a very soft wood that can be bought from model shops. Medium-density fibre-board, or MDF, is a manmade wood. Wear a mask when sawing as it produces a fine dust.

velcro spots

fabric

matchsticks

coloured paper

strong glue

safety pin *cork*

newspaper

sticky stars

cord

rope

balsa wood

masking tape

MDF (fiberboard)

screw eyes

electrical tape

spray paint

enamel paints

double-sided tape

felt

paper bauble

stuffing

paints

bottle top

buttons

varnish

thread

squeaker

dowel

pipe-cleaners

ribbon roses

poppers (snap fasteners)

zip (zipper)

ribbon

paper fasteners

polymer clay

shoelaces

PVA (white) glue

fringing

card

bottle

embroidery threads

Equipment

These are some of the pieces of equipment used in this book.

Bradawl
This is a tool with a sharp point which is used for making holes in wood or card (cardboard).

Craft knife
More accurate than scissors, use this to cut card (cardboard) in conjuncton with a metal rule. Protect your work surface with a sheet of thick card (cardboard) or a special cutting mat.

Coping saw
This is a special saw with a flexible blade for cutting out awkward shapes of wood.

Fretsaw
This is used to cut small, intricate shapes in wood and plastic. The blade can be removed and inserted in a guide hole, then the saw reassembled to allow you to make cut-out shapes in a piece of wood.

Hole punch
Use this to make neat holes in paper and card.

Iron
This is very useful for patchwork to press open the seams.

Modelling tools
These are used with polymer clay, plasticine and other modelling mediums.

Paintbrushes
Available in a wide range of different sizes – and prices, depending on quality. Keep them in good condition by washing immediately after use.

Pair of compasses
Use these for drawing accurate circles. Alternatively, draw round a cup, saucer, plate or other household object.

Pastry cutters
These are excellent for cutting out shapes from polymer clay and other modelling mediums.

Pinking shears
These cut with a decorative zigzag line and prevent fabric edges from fraying.

Pliers
These are used for cutting and bending wire.

Rolling pin
Use one to roll out polymer clay and other modelling mediums, but keep it for craft use and don't use it again in the kitchen.

Sandpaper
Use this to sand the edges and surfaces of pieces of wood smooth before they are painted.

Scissors
These come in a variety of sizes and it is best to have a pair for cutting paper and one for cutting fabric.

Tapestry needle
This is a large needle with a large head and a blunt point.

Tenon saw
Use a tenon saw to cut large or thick pieces of wood.

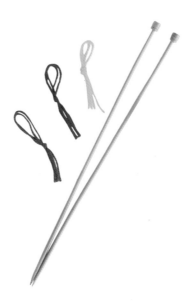

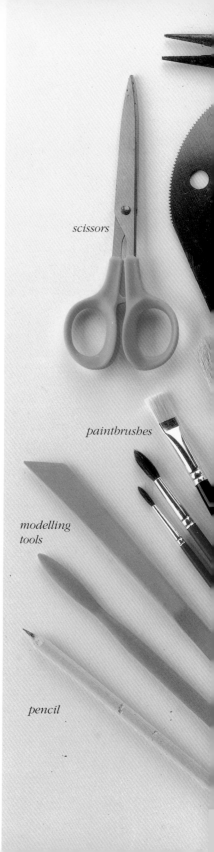

scissors

paintbrushes

modelling tools

pencil

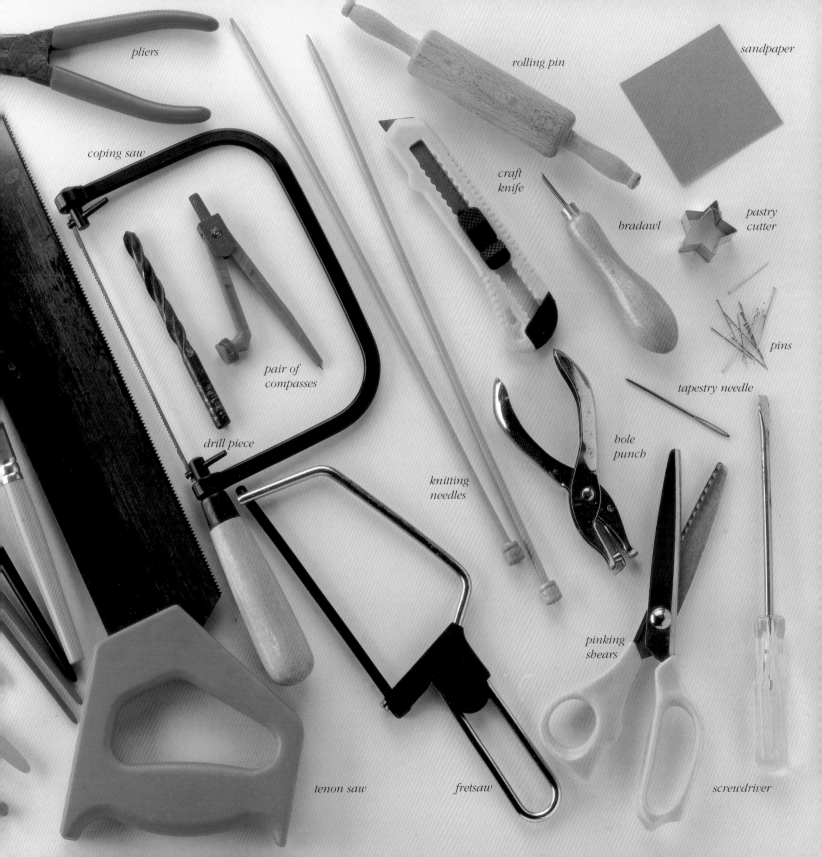

pliers

coping saw

rolling pin

sandpaper

craft knife

bradawl

pastry cutter

pair of compasses

pins

tapestry needle

drill piece

hole punch

knitting needles

tenon saw

fretsaw

pinking shears

screwdriver

TECHNIQUES

Papier-mâché

Papier-mâché is a great way to make something creative and recycle newspapers at the same time.

YOU WILL NEED
newspaper
PVA (white) glue and brush
bowl
water
sandpaper
paintbrush
white emulsion (latex) paint
acrylic paints
varnish and brush

1 Tear up sheets of newspaper into small squares.

2 Pour some PVA (white) glue into a bowl and slowly add water, mixing at the same time to make a smooth paste.

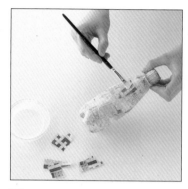
3 Glue the newspaper evenly over a shape or mould and gradually build up layers. Leave the papier-mâché in a warm, dry place to dry overnight, or until it is hard.

4 Rub the papier-mâché lightly with sandpaper to smooth the surface.

5 Paint the papier-mâché with a white undercoat of emulsion (latex) paint. When the undercoat is dry, paint on the colours.

6 When the paint has dried, apply a coat of varnish.

Sanding wood

It is very important to smooth the surface and corners of wood before painting as this will avoid splintering.

■ Use sandpaper to smooth any rough edges on sawn wood.

Drilling wood

When drilling through wood, make sure you protect your work surface adequately.

■ Place an old piece of wood under the piece you want to drill.

Sealing rope ends

Some of the projects use rope and you will need to seal the ends to prevent them unravelling.

■ Carefully burn the rope ends and then put them outside on a stone or concrete surface to cool.

Stuffing soft toys

■ Push stuffing to the ends of toy pieces, using a knitting needle or the end of a wooden spoon to reach small or awkward shapes.

Stitches

Several of the needlework projects use decorative stitches. Some of them you may be familiar with.

French knots

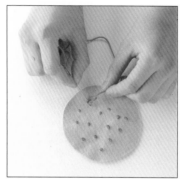 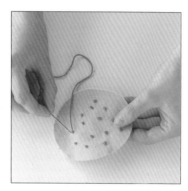

1 Tie a knot at the end of the sewing thread then stitch through to the right side of the fabric. Using the needle, make a knot close to the fabric.

2 Pass the needle back through the fabric again close to the knot.

Blanket stitch

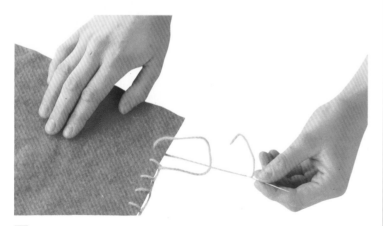

1 Use this stitch for edging fabric to prevent it from fraying. Tie a knot at the end of the sewing thread or wool, and pass it through the fabric from the wrong side. Push the needle through the right side of the fabric 1 cm (½ in) farther on and place the needle over the loop to form a stitch. Repeat.

Bending wire

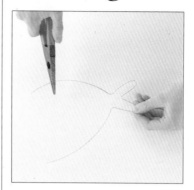 

1 Use a pair of pliers to help you bend a piece of wire into shape.

2 To secure the two ends of the wire together, twist them and press hard with the tips of the pliers.

Making a hole in a can

1 Place a ball of softened plasticine on the can where you want to make a hole then pierce it with a bradawl. This will prevent the bradawl from slipping.

Tracing templates

Some of the projects in this book include templates which you can trace. These instructions show you how to transfer a template to another piece of paper.

Scaling up

Some of the templates in the book are smaller than the actual size you need for the project, so you will need to scale them up. If you have access to a photocopier, you can use it to enlarge the shapes. Otherwise, follow these instructions.

1 Place a piece of tracing paper over the template in the book and draw over the shape with a pencil.

2 Remove the tracing paper and turn it over. Rub over the traced image with a pencil on the reverse side of the tracing paper.

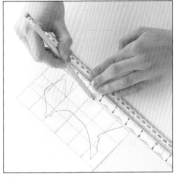

1 Draw a rectangle or square to the nearest 2.5 cm (1 in) round the image you want to enlarge. Divide it into 2.5 cm (1 in) squares.

2 On a separate piece of paper, draw another box as large as you want but in proportion to the first box. Divide it into even squares.

3 Place the tracing paper on top of a piece of card (cardboard) or paper, with the rubbed pencil side facing down. Draw over the shape again to transfer the image.

4 Cut out the shape. You now have a template to draw round. You can use it on paper, card or fabric.

3 Copy the image in the large box, using the squares to help you. Trace the image to make the template.

TEMPLATES

These templates are used in some of the projects in the book. They will need enlarging to the size you want, following the scaling up instructions.

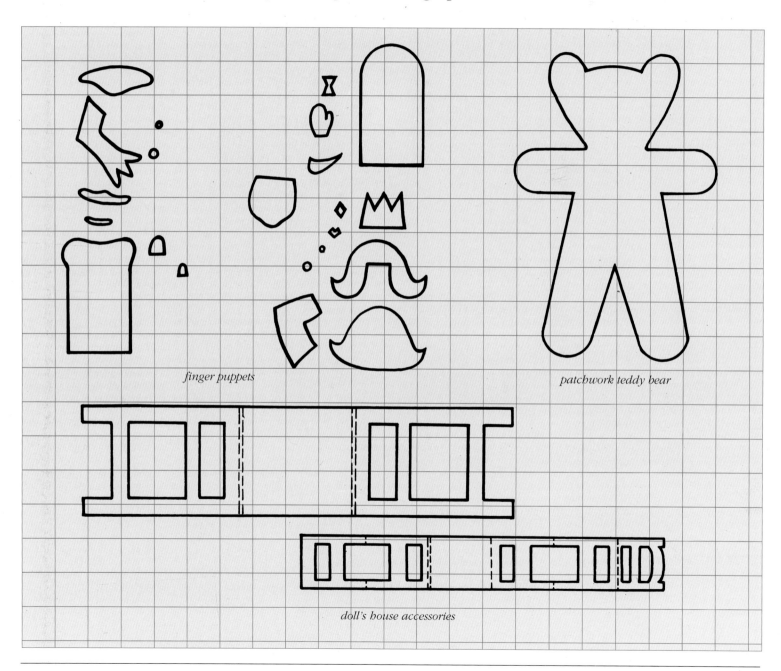

finger puppets

patchwork teddy bear

doll's house accessories

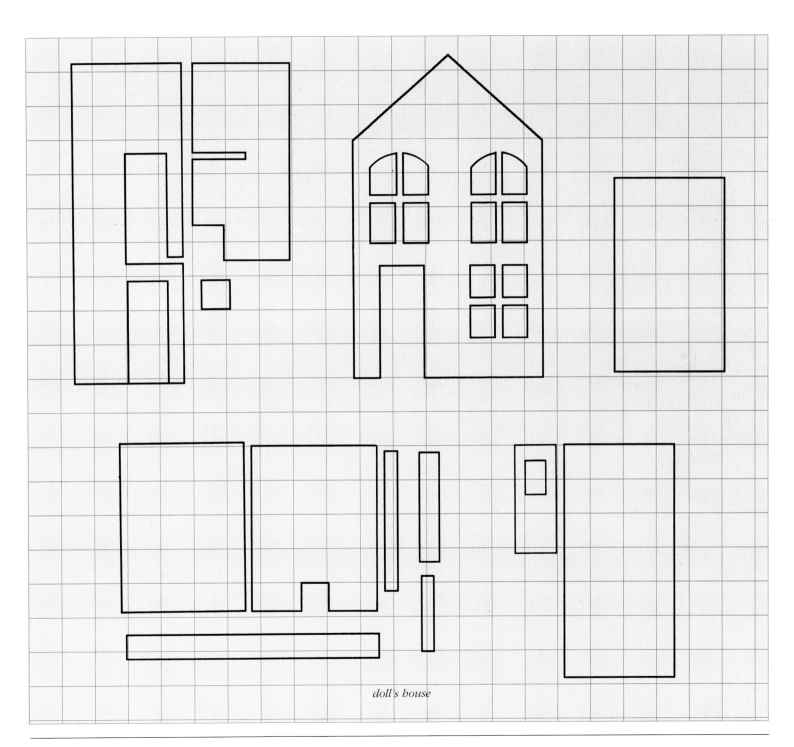

doll's house

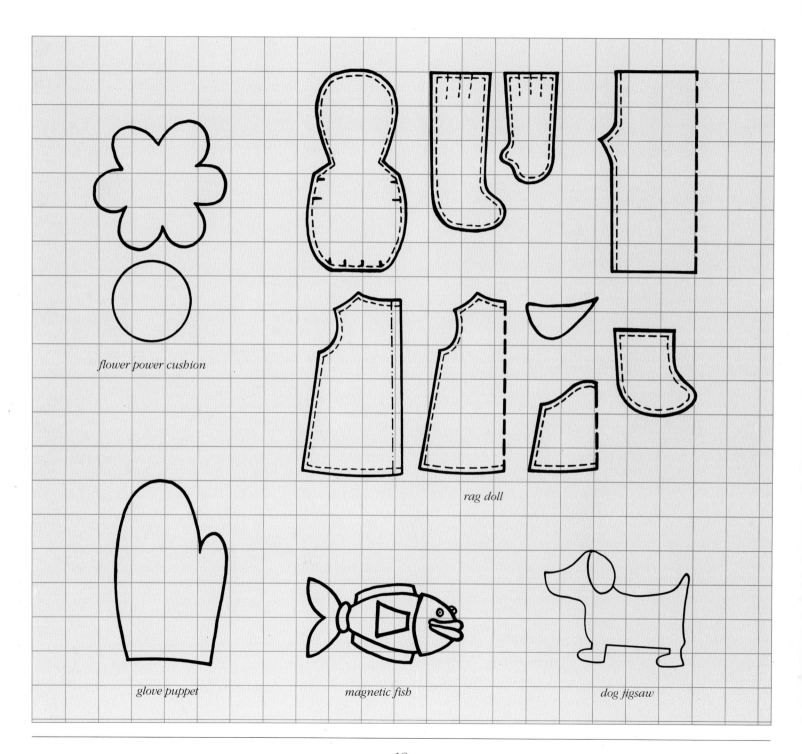

flower power cushion

rag doll

glove puppet

magnetic fish

dog jigsaw

dog and bone mobile

felt picture book

paper fastener puppet

felt noughts and crosses
(tic-tac-toe)

toy bag

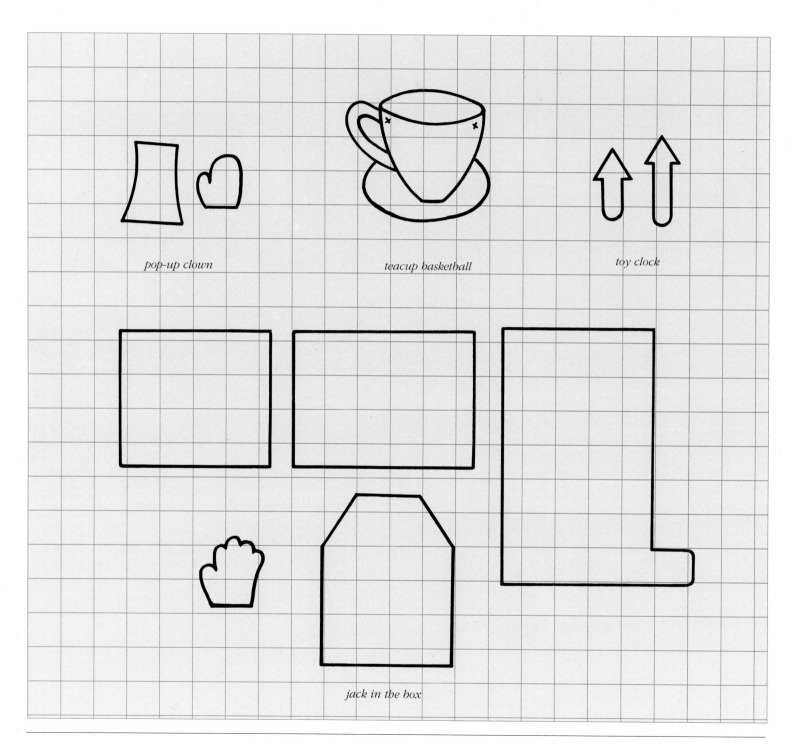

pop-up clown

teacup basketball

toy clock

jack in the box

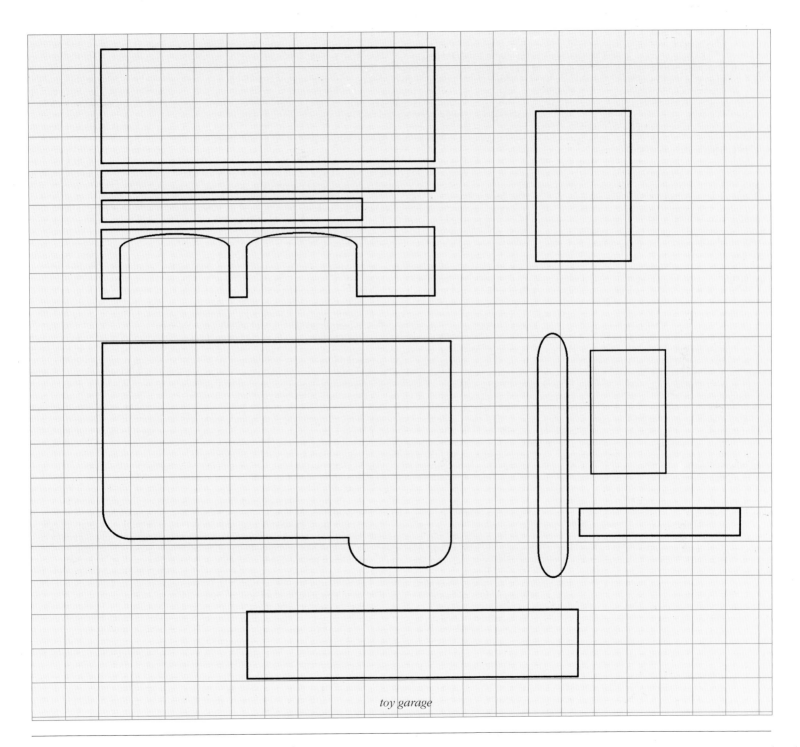

toy garage

FOR THE NURSERY

Squeaky Square

This soft, cuddly toy has a surprise squeaker tucked inside it. You can purchase a squeaker from most craft and haberdashery shops. Using odds and ends of knitting wool (yarn) in bright, cheerful colours, this simple toy is very quick and easy to make.

YOU WILL NEED
knitting wool (yarn), in
  assorted colours
knitting needles
tapestry needle
stuffing
squeaker

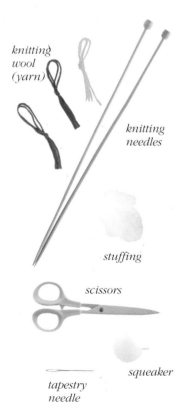

knitting wool (yarn)

knitting needles

stuffing

scissors

squeaker

tapestry needle

1 For each triangle, cast on 11 stitches. Knit every row, decreasing 1 stitch on every second row, until you are left with 2 stitches. Cast off. Make eight triangles in different colours.

2 For the large centre square, cast on 20 stitches. Knit in stocking stitch until you have about 24 rows, or a square. Make two squares in the same colour.

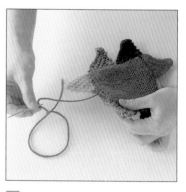

3 Using matching wool (yarn) and a tapestry needle, stitch the two squares together, trapping the triangles round the edge. Leave out one triangle so that there is a gap for the stuffing.

4 Fill the square with the stuffing.

5 Place the squeaker in the middle of the stuffing.

6 Insert the remaining triangle and stitch up the opening.

Decoupage Toy Box

Jazz up an old, or boring, toy box with a splash of paint and some fun cut-outs. Decoupage is very cheap and simple to do – you simply cut out shapes from wrapping paper and paste them on. A layer of varnish means the paper shapes will not rub off and the finished decoration is very hardwearing.

YOU WILL NEED
wooden toy box
sandpaper
emulsion (latex) paint, in
  several colours
paintbrush
wrapping paper
scissors
PVA (white) glue and brush
varnish and brush

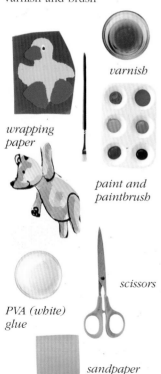

varnish

wrapping paper

paint and paintbrush

PVA (white) glue

scissors

sandpaper

1 First sand down the toy box. Paint the box with emulsion (latex) paint, using a different colour for each side. Leave the paint to dry then apply a second coat.

2 When the paint is dry, cut out shapes from the wrapping paper.

3 Arrange the paper shapes on the box to make a good design. Using the PVA (white) glue, paste them in place.

4 When the glue is dry, varnish the box and fill with toys.

Toy Bag

This bag is a real star! It is big enough to store plenty of toys in at home or if you are going out for the day. Position the star so that it will be in the centre of one side of the bag when the fabric is folded in half.

YOU WILL NEED
paper
pencil
scissors
scraps of fabric, for the star
fabric glue and brush
needle and matching sewing
   threads
52 cm x 110 cm (20½ in x 43 in)
   hardwearing fabric
1 m (39 in) coloured tape
1.5 m (59 in) ribbon or cord
safety pin

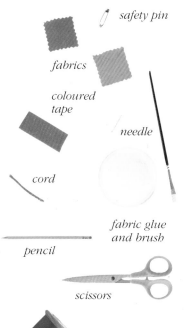

safety pin

fabrics

coloured tape

needle

cord

fabric glue and brush

pencil

scissors

thread

1 Trace the star shape from the template at the front of the book on to paper. Place on the reverse side of a piece of fabric and cut out. Cut out spots in a contrasting colour and glue them on to the right side of the star. Stitch the star on to the right side of the bag fabric.

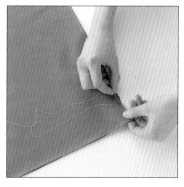

2 With right sides facing, fold the bag fabric in half to make a square. Hand or machine stitch along the sides, leaving a 1 cm (½ in) seam allowance.

3 Fold over the open side by 5 cm (2 in), then stitch round the top of the bag. Turn the bag right side out.

4 Starting at a side seam, pin the tape round the outside of the bag 3 cm (1¼ in) from the top. Fold in the raw ends then stitch along either side of the tape. Attach a safety pin to the end of the ribbon or cord and thread it through the tube. Tie the ends in a knot.

Flower Power Cushion

This checkerboard patchwork cushion is decorated with bright, sunny flowers, just right for small fingers to hold on to. The flowers are attached with velcro so you can move them about to make a different design.

YOU WILL NEED
tracing paper
paper
pencil
scissors
scraps of felt in assorted
  colours, for the flowers
embroidery threads, in assorted
  colours
needle
16 cm (6½ in) Velcro
4 pieces of felt, each 22 cm (8½
  in) square, in different colours
stuffing
2 pieces of fabric, each
  40 cm x 30 cm (16 in x 12 in),
  for the cushion back
40 cm (16 in) square cushion
  pad

stuffing

scissors   *felt*   *pencil*

needle

thread   *velcro*

embroidery   *fabrics*
threads

1 Trace the flower shape from the template at the front of the book. Draw round it four times on different colours of felt. Cut out four circles for the flower centres in contrast colours, and embroider with French knots.

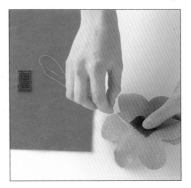

2 Cut the Velcro into four equal pieces. Stitch one half of each piece to the back of each flower, and stitch the other half to the centre of one of the felt squares.

3 Position the flower centres on top of the flowers, trapping a small ball of stuffing in between. Pin in place then stitch round the flower centres.

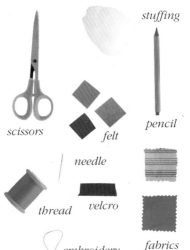

4 For the patchwork, place two of the felt squares together. Hand or machine stitch, leaving a 1 cm (½ in) seam allowance. Join the other two squares the same way, then stitch the two sets of squares together to make a large block.

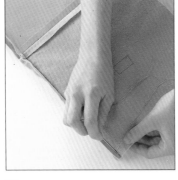

5 Place the two pieces of fabric for the cushion back on the felt block, right sides together. Pin then stitch round all four sides, leaving a 1 cm (½ in) seam allowance. Fold back the raw edges of the back pieces and attach in the seam.

6 Turn the cushion cover right side out and insert the cushion pad. Stitch the opening or insert a zip fastener (zipper). Stick the flowers on to the front.

Pop-up Clown

These popular toys are not difficult to make, and all you need are a piece of dowel and scraps of fabric, felt and trimmings. Simply push the dowel rod and the clown pops up out of nowhere.

YOU WILL NEED
35 cm (13¾ in) dowel
craft knife
small ball of paper
emulsion (latex) paint, in red and another colour
paintbrush
pencil
thin card (cardboard)
scissors
masking tape
felt, in pink and two other colours
fabric glue
paper
needle
matching threads
scraps of fabric
lampshade trimming
ricrac braid
12 cm (4¾ in) ribbon
small pompom

1 Sharpen one end of the dowel into a point, using a craft knife, and push into the paper ball. Paint the dowel rod, then paint a clown's face on the paper ball, using red paint.

2 Draw an 8 cm (3 in) radius semi-circle on to card (cardboard). Cut out, bend into a cone and secure with masking tape. Cut a slightly larger piece of felt and glue on to the cone, folding the edges to the inside.

3 Trace the hand and sleeve templates from the front of the book on to paper. For each hand, fold a piece of pink felt in half and place the template on top. Draw round, stitch along the marked line then cut out, adding a 3 mm (⅛ in) seam allowance. Turn right side out. For the sleeves, fold a piece of fabric in half, right sides together. Continue as for the hands. Tuck the hands in the sleeve openings and stitch.

needle

thread

pompom

pencil

paintbrush

thin card (cardboard)

felt

ricrac braid

fabric glue

craft knife

ribbon

scissors

dowel

fabrics

ball of paper

masking tape

emulsion (latex) paint

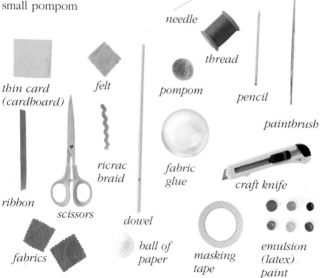

4 For the shirt, cut two pieces of fabric 14 cm x 8 cm (5½ in x 3 in) and place right sides together. Insert the arms at an angle on either side. Stitch the side seams then turn right side out. Hem the top edge.

5 Glue the bottom edge of the shirt to the top of the cone. Glue a piece of lampshade trimming round the top of the cone, covering the raw edges. Decorate with ricrac braid.

6 Push the dowel rod through the cone. Stitch round the top of the shirt in running stitch and pull up the thread to make gathers. Glue to the rod just below the clown's head. Gather the ribbon the same way, stitching along one edge, to make a ruff and glue round the clown's neck. Draw a 4 cm (1½ in) radius semi-circle on to card, cut out, then cut out of felt. Fold in half and stitch the seam to make the hat. Turn right side out and stitch on a pompom. Decorate the bottom of the hat with ricrac braid.

Knitted Cot Toy

Babies love to reach out and grasp these soft, squidgy shapes hanging in a colourful line across a cot or crib. The squares and triangles are easy to knit, and are simply strung on coloured cord. You could add some coloured beads if you like.

YOU WILL NEED
knitting wool (yarn), in assorted colours
knitting needles
tapestry needle
stuffing
cord
scissors

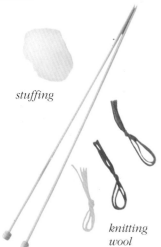

stuffing

knitting wool

knitting needles

scissors

tapestry needle

cord

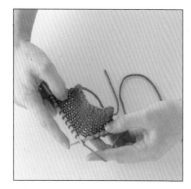

1 For each square, cast on 15 stitches and knit 21 rows in stocking stitch. Cast off. Knit six squares in three different colours. For each triangle, cast on 20 stitches and knit in stocking stitch, decreasing 1 stitch every second row until you are left with 2 stitches. Cast off. Knit four triangles in two different colours. Using matching wool (yarn), stitch the pairs of shapes together, leaving one side open for stuffing.

2 Fill all the shapes with stuffing.

3 Using matching wool, stitch up the openings.

4 Using the tapestry needle, thread the cord through one side of each square and through the straight edge of the triangles. Knot the cord between the shapes.

Knitted Polar Bear

This adorable polar bear is very soft and comforting. His body is knitted in garter stitch throughout and all in one piece.

YOU WILL NEED

50 g (2 oz) white or cream Aran knitting wool (yarn)
4.5 mm (size 7) knitting needles
scissors
tapestry needle
black knitting or tapestry wool (yarn)
stuffing

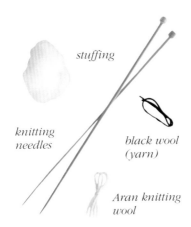

stuffing

knitting needles

black wool (yarn)

Aran knitting wool

tapestry needle

scissors

1 Cast on 40 stitches and knit for 20 rows. Cast off 10 stitches at each end of the next row (20 stitches). Knit 18 rows, then cast on 10 stitches at each end of the next row (40 stitches). Knit 20 rows. Cast off 10 stitches at each end of the next row (20 stitches). Knit 2 rows. Cast off 1 stitch at the end of every second row until you have only 2 stitches. Cast off.

2 Stitch up the hind legs and bottom seam as far as the stomach. Leave a gap for the stuffing. Stitch the nose in black wool. Stitch the front legs. Fill the bear with stuffing then stitch the gap.

3 To make the ears, pinch a small piece of knitting either side of the face. Wrap a piece of wool round each ear and stitch.

4 Stitch the eyes and mouth in black wool.

Patchwork Teddy Bear

Use plain and patterned scraps of fabric to make this colourful teddy bear. Stitch the patches securely together so that the stuffing can't come out – he is sure to get plenty of cuddles. You can stitch the patchwork by hand or using a sewing machine.

YOU WILL NEED
card (cardboard)
ruler
pencil
paper
scissors
assorted fabrics
needle and sewing threads
iron
dressmaker's pins
fabric pen or tailor's chalk
stuffing

fabrics   *scissors*   *ruler*

fabric pen

card (cardboard)

needle   *dressmaker's pins*

sewing thread   *stuffing*   *pencil*

1 Draw a 6 cm (2½ in) square on card (cardboard) and cut out. Place the card on the reverse side of the fabrics and cut out squares. You will need about 80 squares altogether.

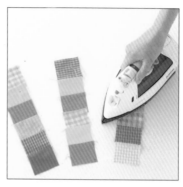

2 With right sides facing, stitch two squares together along one side, leaving a 5 mm (³⁄₁₆ in) seam allowance. Stitch pairs of squares together to make strips. Press the seams with an iron so they lie in one direction.

3 Trace the teddy bear shape from the template at the front of the book and enlarge it on to card or paper to 36 cm (14 in) long. Stitch the strips together to make a piece of patchwork large enough to fit the template.

4 Cut a piece of fabric the same size as the patchwork for the back of the teddy. Pin the two together, right sides facing. Draw round the bear template with a fabric pen or tailor's chalk.

5 Hand or machine stitch round the shape, leaving a 5 cm (2 in) opening for the stuffing. Cut out the teddy bear, leaving a 1 cm (½ in) border. Then turn right side out and fill with stuffing.

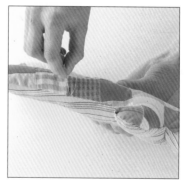

6 Slip stitch the opening.

Dog and Bone Mobile

This witty mobile is great fun. As it swings around in the breeze, the Scottie dog chases the bone and the cat chases the fish! Trace the shapes from the templates supplied, cut them out of card (cardboard) and paint them in bright colours. Hang the rods up before tying on the shapes, as it will be easier to balance them.

YOU WILL NEED
2 x 45 cm (18 in) pieces of
  dowel, 5 mm (³⁄₁₆ in) diameter
saw
sandpaper
drill
craft knife
poster paint, in assorted colours
paintbrush
cord
sticky tape, optional
tracing paper
pencil
card (cardboard)
scissors
single-hole punch
thread, in assorted colours

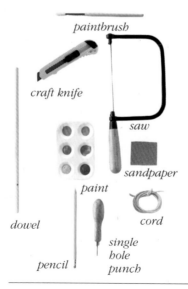

paintbrush
craft knife
saw
sandpaper
paint
dowel
cord
pencil
single hole punch

1 Cut the dowel to size and smooth the ends with sandpaper. Drill a hole in the centre of each dowel rod.

2 Using a craft knife, shave a 'V' shape round the hole on one of the rods. This will help the rods to sit comfortably at right angles to each other. Paint each rod using a different colour and leave to dry.

3 Thread a piece of cord through the holes and tie in a knot either side of the dowel rods. If you have trouble threading the cord through the holes, wrap a piece of sticky tape tightly round the end.

4 Trace the mobile shapes from the templates at the front of the book and transfer them to card (cardboard). Cut out the shapes. Punch a hole on each shape where marked on the templates.

5 Paint the shapes on both sides.

6 Hang up the dowel rods and tie on each shape, using a different coloured thread.

Basic Jigsaw

This simple jigsaw is a good one to practise with before moving on to ones with more pieces. If you do not like drawing, you can glue on a picture from a children's magazine.

YOU WILL NEED
30 cm (12 in) square of card (cardboard)
pencil
paint, in bright colours
paintbrush
craft knife

paintbrush

paint

craft knife

card (cardboard)

pencil

1 Draw a picture on the card (cardboard), using a pencil.

2 Paint the picture, using bright colours. Leave the paint to dry.

3 Turn the card over and divide the square roughly into four. Draw a simple jigsaw shape on each piece.

4 Cut along the lines, using a craft knife for neat edges.

Wire Mobile

These painted wire shapes make a very attractive and unusual mobile. Farmyard animals are the theme here, but you can choose your own design – dinosaurs, fish or wild animals would all look good.

YOU WILL NEED
galvanized steel wire
pliers
enamel paint, in assorted
  colours
paintbrush
threads, in assorted colours
turpentine

*enamel
paint*

pliers

paintbrush

steel wire   *threads*

1 Bend the wire into the shapes you want with the help of a pair of pliers. When you have completed a shape, twist the two ends of the wire firmly together.

2 Paint each shape with enamel paints and hang them up from a piece of thread to dry. Wash the paintbrushes after use with turpentine.

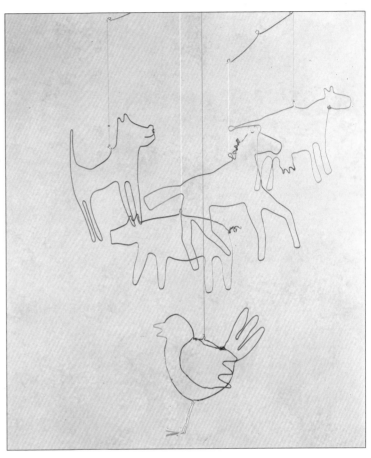

3 Cut three pieces of wire 20 cm (8 in) long. Bend each piece to make a loop in the middle and a loop at either end of the wire.

4 Lay the three pieces of wire on a flat surface and position the shapes round them. Tie the shapes to the loops with coloured threads.

Wooden Boat

Children of all ages will enjoy imaginary journeys in this ocean-liner. Sturdily built in pine, it is too heavy to float in water but it is ideal to play with on land.

YOU WILL NEED
43 cm (17 in) of 8 cm x 5 cm (3 in x 2 in) pine
16 cm (6½ in) of 8 mm (⅝ in) dowel
saw
sandpaper
pencil
drill, with 8 mm (⅝ in) drill bit
wood glue
acrylic paint: pale blue, turquoise, navy, red, white and gold
paintbrush
varnish and brush

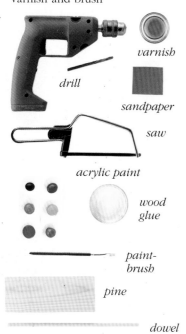

varnish

drill

sandpaper

saw

acrylic paint

wood glue

paint-brush

pine

dowel

pencil

1 Cut the pine into two pieces, 17 cm (6¾ in) and 26 cm (10½ in), and cut the dowel into four equal lengths. Sand the surfaces and corners until smooth.

2 For the portholes, draw a line on the shorter piece of pine along each of the 8 cm (3 in) sides, 2.5 cm (1 in) from the top. Starting at one end, mark with a pencil 3 cm (1½ in), 5 cm (2 in), 7 cm (2¾ in) and so on until you reach 13 cm (5 in). Drill into the pine at these points.

3 For the funnels, mark a line down the centre of one of the 5 cm (2 in) wide sides of the same piece of pine. Mark points at 3.5 cm (1¾ in), 7 cm (2¾ in), 10.5 cm (4¼ in) and 14 cm (5½ in). Drill shallow holes and glue in the dowels.

4 Draw and then cut a pointed bow shape on one end of the large piece of pine, to make the base. Sand until smooth, then glue the shorter piece of pine on top, as shown.

5 Paint the boat, following the colours in the illustration as a guide. If you want to paint a name on the bows, do it at this stage.

6 When the paint is dry, apply a coat of varnish.

Jack in the Box

Lift the lid of this star-studded magician's box for a real surprise! The jolly clown inside is easy to make, using odds and ends of fabric and paper.

YOU WILL NEED
FOR THE BOX
6 mm (¼ in) birch ply
saw
ruler
sandpaper
wood glue and brush
masking tape
brass hinge
undercoat
paintbrush
acrylic paint: blue and gold
varnish and brush
FOR THE CLOWN
tracing paper
pencil
paper
scissors
scraps of fabric
felt
fabric glue
ball of white paper
crayons

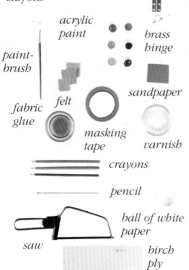

acrylic paint
paint-brush
brass hinge
fabric glue
felt
sandpaper
masking tape
varnish
crayons
pencil
ball of white paper
saw
birch ply

1 Following the diagram, cut out all the pieces for the box. Smooth the surfaces and corners thoroughly with sandpaper. Glue the box together, except for the lid. Hold the pieces in place with masking tape until the glue dries.

2 Attach the lid to the box with the hinge, making sure that the lid closes square to the box. Paint the outside of the box and both sides of the lid with undercoat. Leave to dry.

3 Paint the box and both sides of the lid with blue acrylic paint. When dry, paint on gold stars. When these are dry, varnish the box and lid.

4 Trace the shapes for the clown's clothes from the templates at the front of the book. Cut the shapes out of fabric. Cut out his hands, diamond-shaped buttons and a sawtooth-edge collar and stick on the clothes with fabric glue.

5 Draw a clown face on the ball of paper and colour it in with crayons.

6 Cut a triangle of felt and glue round the head to make a hat. Put some glue on the back of the collar and stick it to the bottom half of the open lid. Apply a large amount of glue to the back of the hat and glue it to the lid directly above the glued collar.

Toy Clock

Recycle your breakfast cereal packet to make a friendly clock, as a fun way of learning how to tell the time. Paint the clock face in sunny day-time colours, and surround it with a night sky painted with stars.

YOU WILL NEED
card (cardboard)
pencil
scissors
emulsion (latex) paint, in assorted colours
paintbrush
craft knife
paper fastener
cereal box
adhesive plastic: blue and yellow
double-sided tape

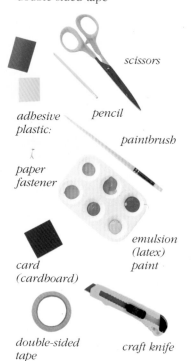

scissors

adhesive plastic:

pencil

paintbrush

paper fastener

emulsion (latex) paint

card (cardboard)

double-sided tape

craft knife

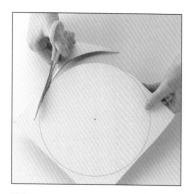

1 Draw round a small plate on to card (cardboard) and cut out. Find the centre of the circle and pierce a hole with the scissors.

2 Paint the card circle in a sunny colour and leave to dry. Paint the numerals in contrast colours and leave to dry.

3 Trace the clock hands from the template at the front of the book on to card and cut out. Paint and attach the arms to the clock with a paper fastener.

4 Cover the cereal box with blue adhesive plastic and smooth down, trying to avoid air bubbles.

5 Stick the clock face on to the box with double-sided tape. Cut out stars from yellow adhesive plastic and stick on to the sides of the box.

6 Stick more stars on the front of the clock round the face.

Activity Blanket

Tiny fingers will love playing with this blanket, and at the same time they will learn how to use zips (zippers), buttons and shoelaces. Make sure all the pieces are securely attached, especially the buttons.

YOU WILL NEED
coloured blanket
tapestry wool (yarn), in bright
  colours
tapestry needle
scissors
coloured zips (zippers)
dressmaker's pins
scraps of contrast-coloured
  blanket or felt
buttons
pompoms
laces

felt

tapestry needle

zip (zipper)

button

pompoms

scissors

laces

tapestry wool

1 Cut the blanket if necessary to the size you want. Fold under the edges and blanket stitch, using contrasting tapestry wool (yarn).

2 Position the zips on the blanket and pin in place. Secure with running stitch, using contrasting tapestry wool.

3 Cut out simple shapes, such as squares, circles and triangles, from coloured blanket or felt. Cut a slit in the centre of each shape for a button to go through. Stitch the buttons on to the blanket and fasten on the shapes.

4 Sew on pompoms and laces as more shapes to play with.

Felt Picture Book

The great thing about this colourful book is that you don't have to worry about the pages getting torn or crumpled. Make up a bedtime story to go with the pictures, or invent your own story and pictures.

YOU WILL NEED
paper
pencil
scissors
scraps of felt, for the pictures
5 pieces of felt, 6 cm (2½ in) square, in different colours
fabric glue and brush
6.5 cm (2¾ in) strip of felt, for the spine
embroidery thread
needle

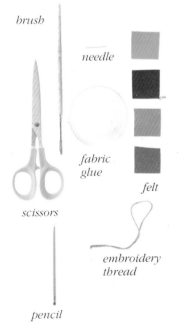

brush

needle

fabric glue

felt

scissors

embroidery thread

pencil

1 Trace the shapes from the templates at the front of the book on to paper and cut out. Lay the paper shapes on scraps of different coloured felt and cut out.

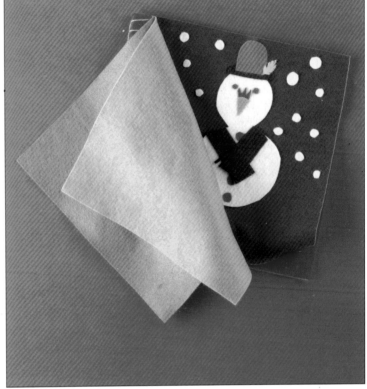

2 Position the felt shapes on the felt squares to make the pictures. Glue in place. Leave the glue to dry.

3 Place the felt squares on top of each other, with the pictures facing upwards. Place a plain felt square on top. Cut the felt spine to the length of the book, fold in half and glue round the edge, trapping all the pages inside. Leave to dry.

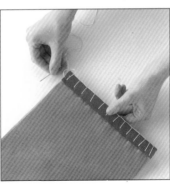

4 To secure the spine, stitch through all the layers with embroidery thread, using a contrasting colour and neat blanket stitch.

Bottle Maracas

Hold one of these in each hand and shake them in time to music – they make a great sound! For instructions on how to cover the bottles with papier-mâché, see the Techniques section at the beginning of the book.

YOU WILL NEED
FOR THE PAPIER-MÂCHÉ
newspaper
bowl
water
PVA (white) glue and brush
FOR THE MARACAS
2 small, empty plastic bottles
emulsion (latex) paint, in
   assorted colours
paintbrush
buttons
strong glue
A4 (11¾ in x 8½ in) sheet of
   paper
100 g (4 oz) lentils or other
   dried pulses (legumes)
2 pieces of balsa wood, each
   12 cm (4¾ in) long
craft knife
coloured electrical tape

 buttons

paint

PVA (white) glue

brush

newspaper

electrical tape

lentils

strong glue

balsa wood

 *craft knife*

plastic bottle

1 Make sure the bottles are clean and dry. Cover both bottles with two layers of papier-mâché.

2 When the papier-mâché is dry, paint the bottles all over in a base colour. Leave to dry.

3 Paint colourful patterns on top of the base colour. Leave the paint to dry.

4 Glue buttons round the bottom of the bottles with strong glue. Leave to dry.

5 Roll the sheet of paper into a cone and fit into the top of one of the bottles. Pour half the lentils or pulses into the bottle. Repeat for the second bottle.

6 Shave one end of the pieces of balsa wood with a craft knife until they fit snugly into the bottles.

7 Glue the balsa wood into the bottles with strong glue. When dry, wind coloured tape round the handles, and paint the ends of the handles.

Number Blocks

Turn adding, subtracting and dividing sums into a game with these chunky wooden cubes. They can also be piled on top of each other like building blocks. Store them in a box decorated to match.

YOU WILL NEED
15 cm x 15 cm x 5 cm
  (6 in x 6 in x 2 in) wood
ruler
saw
sandpaper
emulsion (latex) or acrylic paint,
  in assorted colours
paintbrush
varnish and brush

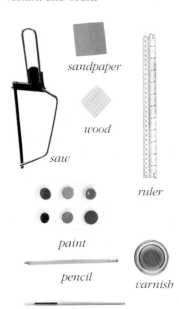

sandpaper

wood

saw

ruler

paint

pencil

varnish

paintbrush

1 Measure the piece of wood into nine cubes, and cut out. Smooth the surfaces and edges thoroughly with sandpaper.

2 Paint the cubes, using a different colour for each side. Leave the paint to dry.

3 Paint on numbers and mathematical signs in contrasting colours. When the paint has dried, varnish the blocks.

4 Find or make a box the right size to fit all the blocks in. Paint to match, and varnish.

Building Block House

This pretty house is made out of building blocks, so putting it together is like doing a jigsaw puzzle. Each time you build the house, you can move the windows round to give a different colour scheme.

YOU WILL NEED
15 cm x 15 cm x 5 cm
  (6 in x 6 in x 2 in) wood
pencil
ruler
saw
sandpaper
emulsion (latex) or acrylic paint,
  in assorted colours
paintbrush
20 cm x 10 cm (8 in x 4 in)
  piece of wood, for the roof
varnish and brush

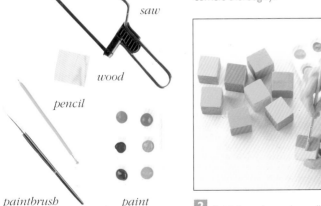

saw

wood

pencil

paintbrush   *paint*

sandpaper

varnish

ruler

1 Measure and then cut nine cubes from the wood. Sand the surfaces and corners thoroughly.

2 Paint the cubes, using a different colour for each side. Leave the paint to dry.

3 Take the piece of wood for the roof and saw off each side at a 45° angle. Sand the surface and corners thoroughly. Paint the roof then, when dry, paint on the roof tiles.

4 Paint a door and windows on some of the cubes. Varnish all the building blocks and the roof.

Dumper Truck

All sorts of heavy loads can be carried in this sturdy wooden lorry.

YOU WILL NEED
65 cm (26 in) of 10 cm x 1 cm
 (4 in x ½ in) pine
39.5 cm (15½ in) of 6 cm x 1 cm
 (2½ in x ½ in) pine
ruler
pencil
saw
sandpaper
PVA (white) glue and brush
60 cm (24 in) of 1 cm x 1 cm
 (½ in x ½ in) pine lipping
drill, with 5 mm (¼ in) and
 4 mm (³⁄₁₆ in) drill bits
9.5 cm (3¾ in) of 5 cm (2 in)
 square pine
9 cm (3½ in) of 5 cm (2 in)
 triangle pine
23 cm (9 in) of 4 mm (³⁄₁₆ in)
 diameter dowel
10 cm (4 in) of 5 cm (2 in)
 diameter dowel
emulsion (latex) or acrylic paint,
 in assorted colours
paintbrush
varnish and brush

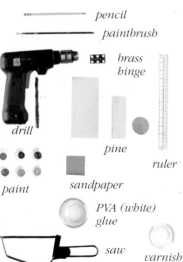

pencil
paintbrush
brass hinge
drill
pine
ruler
paint
sandpaper
PVA (white) glue
saw
varnish

1 Cut two 29 cm (11½ in) lengths of 10 cm x 1 cm (4 in x ½ in) pine. Cut the 6 cm x 1 cm (2½ in x ½ in) pine into two pieces, 30 cm (12 in) and 9.5 cm (3¾ in). Sand all the edges. Glue together to make the back of the truck.

2 Cut the 1 cm x 1 cm (½ in x ½ in) lipping in half. Holding the two pieces together, drill a 5 mm (¼ in) hole in either end. Glue to the underside of the remaining piece of 10 cm x 1 cm (4 in x ½ in) pine. Leave to dry.

3 Glue the square and triangular wood to make the cabin. Glue this to one end of the piece made in step 2. Attach the hinge to the back end of the truck base and to the bottom of the storage section.

4 Cut four 2.5 cm (1 in) lengths from the 5 cm (2 in) diameter dowel, for the wheels. Drill a hole in the centre of each halfway through. Cut the 4 mm (³⁄₁₆ in) dowel in half. Glue one end of each piece into two of the wheels.

5 Paint the truck and the wheels. When the paint is dry, apply a coat of varnish.

6 Assemble the wheels by pushing the 4 mm (³⁄₁₆ in) dowel through the two sets of holes under the truck. Glue the remaining two wheels on to either end.

Dog Jigsaw

It is very easy to make your own simple, large-scale jigsaw. A template for the dog is supplied but you could also make a jigsaw of your own pet, or another favourite animal, or choose a completely different shape.

YOU WILL NEED
pencil
card (cardboard)
craft knife
acrylic paint, in assorted colours
paintbrush
ruler
about 20 self-adhesive Velcro spots
40 cm x 30 cm (16 in x 12 in) piece of adhesive-backed felt
45 cm x 35 cm (18 in x 14 in) piece of thick cardboard

card (cardboard)

adhesive-backed felt

paintbrush

acrylic paint

ruler

scissors

Velcro spots

pencil

craft knife

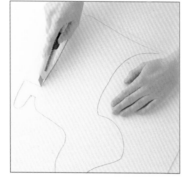

1 Enlarge the template at the front of the book to 36 cm (14 in) long. Draw round the dog shape on to card (cardboard) and cut out with a craft knife.

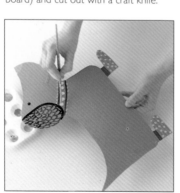

2 Paint the dog as illustrated, or using your own colours. Leave the paint to dry.

3 Using a ruler, divide the dog into four or five simple pieces. Cut along the lines with the craft knife. Stick three or four Velcro spots on the back of each piece.

4 Make his base by placing the thick card in the middle of the felt, fold over the edges and stick down.

Refrigerator magnets

There are several modelling materials you could use in this project, such as polymer clay which can be purchased from craft and hobby shops. Whichever material you use, it is important to follow the instructions on the packet.

YOU WILL NEED
modelling medium
rolling pin (optional)
modelling tools (optional)
acrylic paints, in
  assorted colours
paintbrush
magnets
strong glue

paintbrush

modelling medium

magnets

paints

strong glue

modelling tools

rolling pin

1 To make the teapot and the cups and saucers, mould each shape with your fingers, adding small pieces of the modelling medium for the details. If you are using polymer clay, you will need to roll it out first and cut out the shapes with a modelling tool.

2 For the snail, roll out a length of modelling medium approximately 15 cm (6 in) long and coil it round. Add on small pieces for the antennae.

3 Paint the shapes and leave the paint to dry. If you are using polymer clay, you do not need to paint it.

4 Glue a magnet on to the back of each shape with strong glue. Leave the glue to harden before placing the magnets on the refrigerator.

Squeaky Floor Cushion

Make a large, comfortable cushion for sitting or lying on the floor but watch out – this joke cushion has a squeaker hidden underneath each of the coloured spots! The back of the cushion is made in two pieces so that you can insert a cushion pad.

YOU WILL NEED
scraps of fabric
scissors
6 squeakers
needle and matching sewing
  threads
paper
pencil
felt, in 6 different colours
62 cm (25 in) square of plain-
  coloured fabric, for the front
2 pieces of fabric 62 cm x 40 cm
  (25 in x 16 in), for the back
60 cm (24 in) square
  cushion pad

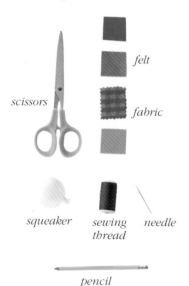

scissors

felt

fabric

squeaker   *sewing thread*   *needle*

pencil

1 Cut out twelve 6 cm (2½ in) squares of fabric. Stitch the squares together in pairs round three sides. Insert a squeaker inside each square then stitch up the openings.

2 Draw round a mug or tumbler to make a round paper template. Place the template on the felt and cut out six circles.

3 Arrange the felt circles on the square of plain fabric to make a nice design. Place a fabric-covered squeaker under each circle then stitch round the edge.

4 Turn under a double hem along one long edge of each piece of fabric for the cushion back. Hand or machine stitch in place.

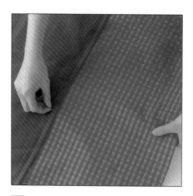

5 With right sides facing, lay the two back pieces on top of the cushion front so that they overlap slightly. Hand or machine stitch round all four sides.

6 Turn the cushion cover right side out and insert the cushion pad.

Sunny Flower Blackboard

This novel blackboard should make sums and spelling more fun! Make it as large as you like, to fit your wall. If you have an electric jig-saw you can use it to cut out the flower shape, otherwise use a coping saw.

YOU WILL NEED
MDF (fiberboard)
pencil
saw
sandpaper
emulsion (latex) paint, in
  assorted colours
paintbrush
blackboard paint
bradawl
2 screw eyes
string

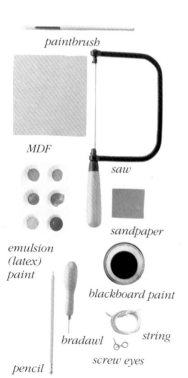

paintbrush

MDF

saw

sandpaper

emulsion (latex) paint

blackboard paint

bradawl

string

screw eyes

pencil

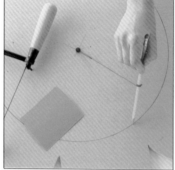

1 Draw the flower on the wood and cut out. For the centre, use a pencil and string to draw a circle, as shown, or draw round a plate. Smooth the edges with sandpaper.

2 Paint each petal a different colour, leave to dry then paint a second coat. Leave to dry.

3 Paint the centre of the flower with two coats of blackboard paint. Leave to dry.

4 Turn the flower over. Mark two points, one on each side, and make small holes with a bradawl. Screw the screw eyes into the holes until they are tight. Tie a piece of string securely to each screw eye, allowing some slack for hanging.

Village Play Mat

Make this waterproof, hardwearing mat any size you like, depending on your floor space. Adhesive plastics are ideal for the stick-on shapes, but if these are not available use oil cloth and glue it on with strong glue.

YOU WILL NEED
large piece of oil cloth
adhesive plastic or oil cloth, in assorted colours including black
scissors
strong glue and brush, optional

strong glue

oil cloth

adhesive plastic

brush

scissors

1 Cut strips of black for the roads and position on the large piece of oil cloth. Stick in place, using glue if necessary. Cut thin strips 4 cm (1½ in) long in grey or white, and stick down the middle of the roads.

2 Cut out green shapes for the trees and brown shapes for tree trunks. Stick small spots on some of the trees for apples.

3 Cut squares and rectangles for the buildings. Stick on door, window and roof shapes. Cut a round blue shape for the pond and stick fish shapes on top.

4 Position all the shapes on the mat then stick in place. Add a few clumps of rushes round the edge of the pond. If you are using glue, leave to dry.

Toy Garage

This is the perfect place to park toy cars at night, and to play with them during the day. It is great fun speeding up and down the steep ramp.

YOU WILL NEED

1.2 m x 50 cm x 6 mm (1¼ yd x 20 in x ¼ in) birch plywood
pencil
fretsaw or bandsaw
1.5 m x 3.4 cm x 8 mm (1¾ yd x 1⅓ in x ⅜ in) pine
60 cm (24 in) half-round beading
sandpaper
wood glue and brush
masking tape
white undercoat
emulsion (latex) paint, in assorted colours
paintbrush

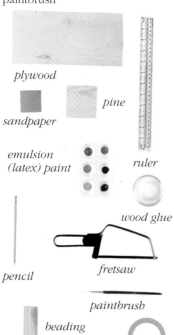

plywood

sandpaper

pine

emulsion (latex) paint

ruler

wood glue

pencil

fretsaw

paintbrush

beading

masking tape

1 Trace the garage shapes from the template at the front of the book. Transfer them on to the plywood and cut out. Cut the pine into one length each of 39.5 cm (15½ in), 39.2 cm (15⅜ in) and two lengths of 15 cm (6 in). Cut the half-round beading into six lengths of 10 cm (4 in). Tilt the bandsaw table to 45 degrees and cut an angle along the top and bottom of the ramp. Sandpaper all the pieces thoroughly.

2 Glue the four wall sections on to the base, using masking tape to hold them in position while the glue dries.

3 Glue the six pieces of half-round beading to the uprights, to act as pillars.

5 Glue the ramp into place on the top and bottom levels.

6 Paint the garage with undercoat, then paint on the colours. Finally, varnish the garage.

4 Glue the pine lengths round the roof. Place them against the facing edges of the roof, supported by the pillars.

Playtime Stage

Dress up a cardboard box with coloured paper, pretty fabric and paint and, hey presto, you have a theatre! The princess and the frog finger puppets are giving this performance, and many other toys will want to take part.

YOU WILL NEED
large cardboard box
pencil
ruler
craft knife
masking tape
paint
paintbrush
fabric, 50 cm (20 in) x the
  height of the box
scissors
PVA (white) glue and brush
coloured paper, in 3 colours

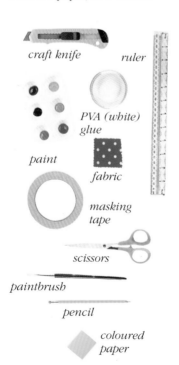

craft knife *ruler*

PVA (white) glue

paint

fabric

masking tape

scissors

paintbrush

pencil

coloured paper

1 Draw a rectangle on the top half of one side of the box and cut out, using a craft knife. Cut away the back of the box and half the base, leaving enough support to allow it to stand. Strengthen the joins with masking tape.

2 Paint the inside of the box a bright colour. Leave the paint to dry.

3 Cut the fabric in half to make two curtains 25 cm (10 in) wide. Fold into pleats along the top of each curtain and secure by wrapping with masking tape. Glue the curtains either side of the stage front.

4 Cut a piece of coloured paper the width of the stage and 10 cm (4 in) deep. Mark a line 2 cm (¾ in) from the edge and score with scissors so that it will fold. Cut a zigzag line along the bottom edge and glue to the theatre.

5 Measure the sides and top of the theatre and cut out pieces of coloured paper to fit. Glue in place and leave to dry.

6 Cut wiggly strips of paper in a contrasting colour. Glue on to the front of the stage.

Finger Puppets

These two favourite fairytale characters, the princess and the frog, are very easy to make. The princess puppet is made the same way as the frog. Be careful not to use too much glue and allow the glue to dry before sticking on the next shape.

YOU WILL NEED
paper
pencil
scissors
felt, in colours as illustrated
fabric glue and brush

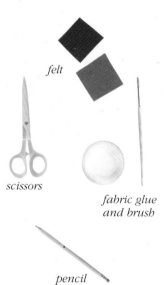

felt

scissors

fabric glue and brush

pencil

1 Trace the princess and frog shapes from the templates at the front of the book on to paper. Cut the shapes out of felt, choosing a suitable colour for each piece. Glue the two pieces for the base together, leaving the bottom edge open.

2 To make the frog, glue the eyes and arms on to one side of the puppet.

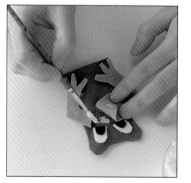

3 Leave the glue to dry then add the large mouth shape. Leave to dry.

4 Finally add the details for the fingers, mouth and nostrils

Glove Puppets

Make different puppets for each hand, so they can perform together or in the theatre with the finger puppets. If your child's hands are a different size to the template, simply draw round the hand and add a generous seam allowance.

YOU WILL NEED
pencil
paper
scissors
felt, blanket or wool fabric
embroidery thread: blue and red
tapestry needle
knitting wool (yarn)
buttons

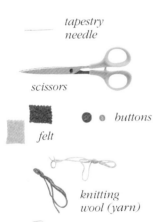

tapestry
needle

scissors

buttons

felt

knitting
wool (yarn)

embroidery
thread

pencil

1 Trace the glove template from the front of the book on to paper and cut out. Draw round it on to the felt or fabric and cut out two glove shapes. Embroider blue eyes and a red mouth on one shape.

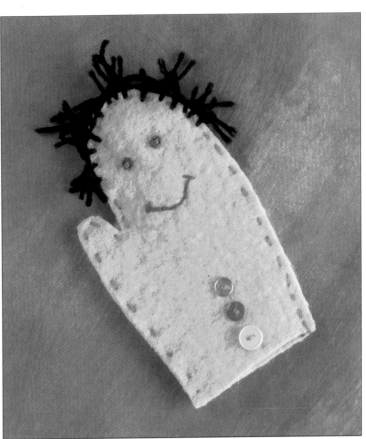

2 Place the two shapes together, wrong sides together, and stitch round the edge in running stitch. Leave the bottom edge open.

3 For the hair, stitch short lengths of knitting wool (yarn) through the top of the glove and knot.

4 Finally stitch a row of buttons down the centre front.

Paper Fastener Puppet

It's amazing what you can do with basic, everyday equipment such as paper fasteners. Here they are used to joint the limbs of this smartly dressed puppet, so that you can make him wave and dance. Hang him up on the back of a child's bedroom door or on the wall.

YOU WILL NEED
card (cardboard)
pencil
scissors
paint, in assorted colours
paintbrush
4 paper fasteners
embroidery thread
electrical tape

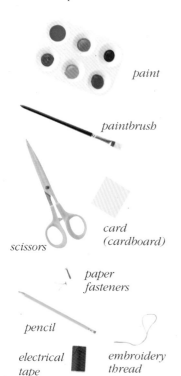

paint

paintbrush

scissors

card (cardboard)

paper fasteners

pencil

electrical tape

embroidery thread

1 Trace the puppet templates from the front of the book. You will need two arms and two legs. Draw round the shapes on to card (cardboard) and cut out, using scissors.

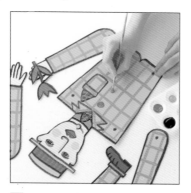

2 Paint the shapes in background colours and leave to dry. Then paint the details of the man's checked suit and his face.

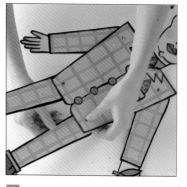

3 Make holes on the arms and legs, as shown on the templates. Make four holes on the body, as shown. Attach the limbs to the body with the paper fasteners.

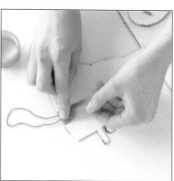

4 Using tape, stick a double length of embroidery thread behind the top of the puppet's head so that you can hang him up.

Mexican Clay Doll

This doll is made in the traditional Mexican way, with the arms and legs tied to the body with threads. It is very fragile so this toy is best kept on a shelf as an ornament.

YOU WILL NEED
self-hardening clay
modelling tool
acrylic paint, in assorted colours
paintbrush
strong embroidery thread

self-hardening clay

embroidery thread

acrylic paints

paintbrush

modelling tools

1 Shape the body, arms and legs out of the clay. Make sure the arms and legs are the same size. Lay the pieces on a board or other flat surface.

2 Using a modelling tool, pierce a hole at the top of each limb and at each corner of the body. Leave to dry in a warm place overnight, or as directed on the packet.

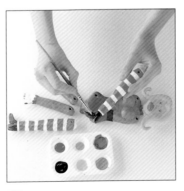

3 When the pieces have fully hardened, paint them in bright colours. Leave the paint to dry.

4 Tie the arms and legs to the body with lengths of thread, leaving enough slack for them to move freely.

Rag Doll

Every little girl needs a calico doll like this as a best friend. First make the doll, then make her a special outfit to wear, such as a dress and matching pantaloons.

YOU WILL NEED
paper
pencil
scissors
50 cm x 1 m (20 in x 39 in)
  calico
matching sewing thread
needle
knitting needle, optional
scraps of felt: blue and pink
embroidery thread: blue, pink
  and red
tapestry needle
yellow knitting wool (yarn)
ribbon

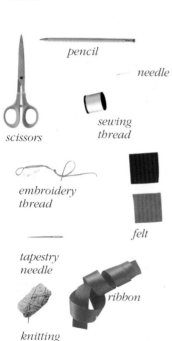

pencil

needle

scissors

sewing thread

embroidery thread

felt

tapestry needle

ribbon

knitting wool

1 Trace the doll templates from the front of the book and cut out. Fold the calico in half and draw round the shapes. Cut the body shape out once and the arm and leg shapes twice. Stitch the shapes together in pairs, leaving an opening in each for stuffing.

2 Turn all the pieces right side out and fill with stuffing until firm. Use a knitting needle if necessary to push the stuffing into the furthest corners. Slip stitch the openings to close.

3 Pinch the tops of the arms and legs, then stitch.

4 Stitch the arms and legs securely to the body.

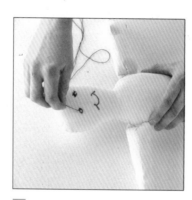

5 Cut two small circles out of blue felt for the doll's eyes, and two slightly larger circles out of pink felt for her cheeks. Stitch on to her face, using embroidery threads. Embroider her mouth in red in running stitch.

6 Stitch short lengths of yellow wool (yarn) through the top of the doll's head, tying each in a knot close to her head. Then give her hair a neat trim. Tie the ribbon in a bow and stitch in position as shown.

Rag Doll's Dress

The simple dress is decorated with a double felt collar and ribbon roses, which you can buy in craft and needlework shops. It fastens at the back with a row of poppers, so is ideal for dressing and undressing the doll.

YOU WILL NEED
paper
pencil
scissors
50 cm x 1 m (20 in x 39 in) dress fabric
matching sewing thread
needle
ribbon roses
poppers (snap fasteners)

dress fabric

scissors

ribbon roses

needle

poppers (snap fasteners)

pencil

sewing thread

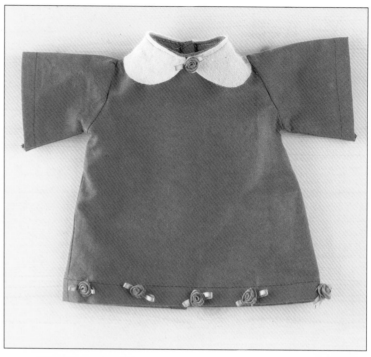

1 Trace the dress templates from the front of the book on to paper. Fold the fabric in half, place the pattern piece for the front on the fold and cut out. Cut two sleeves and two back pieces. Stitch the sleeve seams and hem the cuffs. Leave 6 mm (¼ in) seam allowance.

2 Stitch the two back pieces to the front piece, right sides together. Turn under 6 mm (¼ in) and hem.

3 Right sides together, stitch the shoulder seams. Turn the dress right side out. Place the sleeves through the armholes as shown and tack (baste) in position, then stitch.

4 Turn over 6 mm (¼ in) round the neck edge to the right side and stitch. Trace the collar template on to paper and cut out twice from felt. Stitch both collars round the neck edge. Decorate the dress with ribbon roses. Turn the raw edges of the back opening under 2 cm (¾ in) to the wrong side and stitch. Stitch poppers (snap fasteners) to either side of the opening at the back.

Rag Doll's Pantaloons and Boots

Make the pantaloons in plain or patterned fabric to contrast with the rag doll's dress. Her boots are easily made out of scraps of fabric.

YOU WILL NEED
paper
pencil
scissors
matching sewing threads
needle
FOR THE BOOTS
scrap of fabric
FOR THE PANTALOONS
70 cm (27½ in) x 1 m (39 in) dress fabric
60 cm (24 in) narrow elastic
safety pin

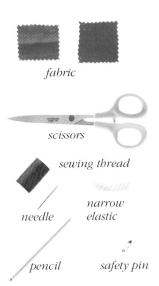

fabric

scissors

sewing thread

needle   *narrow elastic*

pencil   *safety pin*

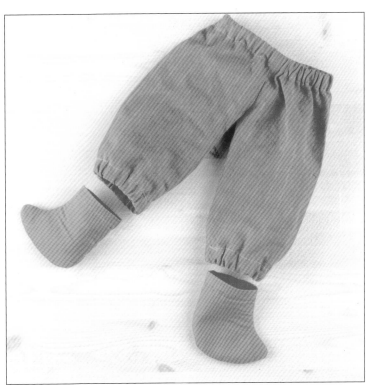

1 Trace the boot template from the front of the book on to paper. Fold a small piece of fabric in half, draw round the shape twice and cut out. Stitch two boot shapes together, right sides facing, leaving the top open. Repeat for the other boot.

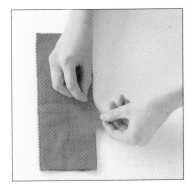

2 Trace the pantaloons template. Fold the fabric in half, right sides facing, then place the pattern piece on the fold as marked. Cut out twice. Keeping the fabric folded in half, hand or machine stitch along the inside leg.

3 Turn one pantaloon leg right side out and place inside the other leg, with raw edges matching along the crotch seam. Stitch the crotch seam and turn right side out. Fold the waist edge over 3 cm (1¼ in) to the wrong side then stitch round the waist 1 cm (½ in) from the top, leaving a small opening. Repeat at the bottom of each leg.

4 Cut the elastic into one piece of 30 cm (12 in) and two pieces of 15 cm (6 in). Pin a safety pin to one end of the long piece and thread it through the waistband. Pull both ends to gather the waist and stitch firmly together. Repeat for the pantaloon legs.

Doll's House

This pretty little house is a real dream house, ready to furnish and decorate. The whole front of the house is attached with a hinge so that you can open it and see inside. Instead of buying expensive doll's house furniture, make your own using matchboxes and card (cardboard).

YOU WILL NEED
1.8 m x 37 cm (2⅛ yd x 15 in) of 6 mm (¼ in) birch plywood
4 cm x 2.2 cm (1½ in x ⅞ in) pine
pencil
bandsaw
drill
fretsaw
sandpaper
wood glue and brush
masking tape
3 cm (1¼ in) of 12 mm (⁹⁄₁₆ in) diameter dowel
white emulsion (latex) paint, as undercoat
emulsion (latex) paint, in pastel colours
2 brass hinges
screws

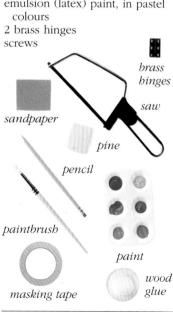

brass hinges

saw

sandpaper

pine

pencil

paintbrush

paint

masking tape

wood glue

1 Cut out the templates from the front of the book from the plywood. Tilt the bandsaw table to 45° and cut either side of the roof panels and the top of each side wall at an angle.

2 Trace the details from the template on to the front of the house. Drill a hole through each separate area and cut out the windows and door using a fretsaw. Sand any rough edges.

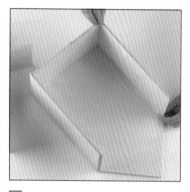

3 Glue the interior wall and upper floor together at right angles. Glue the back wall and both side walls to the base. Use masking tape to hold the pieces in position while the glue dries.

4 Glue the interior fittings and the roof support in place then glue the roof panels in position. Glue the chimney stack to the outside wall.

5 Drill a large hole through the top board of the chimney and fit the dowel into it. Glue to the top of the chimney stack. Stick the door, windowsills and gable to the front.

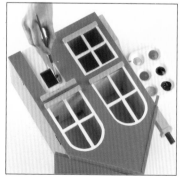

6 Paint the house with white emulsion (latex) paint as an undercoat. When dry, paint on colours. Finish with varnish. Attach the front to the main part of the house, with the hinges and screws.

Doll's House Furniture

You can furnish your doll's house very inexpensively, using matchboxes, corks, bottle tops and other odds and ends.

YOU WILL NEED
scissors
masking tape
glue
felt
stuffing
embroidery thread
needle
7 small matchboxes
coloured paper
matches
lampshade fringing
large matchbox
craft knife
emulsion (latex) or acrylic paint
paintbrush
6 paper fasteners
2 plastic bottle tops
2 corks
buttons

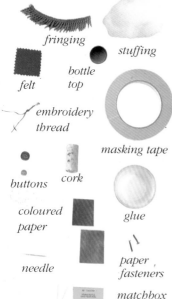

fringing

stuffing

bottle top

felt

embroidery thread

buttons   *cork*

masking tape

coloured paper

glue

needle

paper fasteners

matchbox

1 CUSHIONS: For each cushion, cut two 4 cm (1½ in) squares of felt. Trap a small amount of stuffing between them then stitch round the edge, using embroidery thread. Stitch a button on each side.

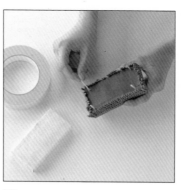

2 BED: Fasten three matchboxes together in a row with masking tape. Cover with coloured paper. Pierce a hole in each corner underneath the bed and place a match without a head in each hole. Cut a length of fringing to fit around the bed and glue in place.

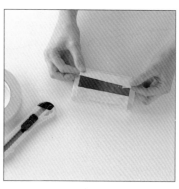

3 WARDROBE: Cut two holes for doors in the front of a large matchbox and reinforce with masking tape.

4 Cover the wardrobe doors with coloured paper then paint the rest of the box. Insert a paper fastener through each door as a handle. Glue the bottle tops on the bottom.

5 THE CHEST OF DRAWERS: Stick four small matchboxes together with masking tape.

6 Glue a piece of coloured paper over the chest-of-drawers then paint the drawers. When the paint is dry, pierce a paper fastener through the centre of each drawer. Cut the corks in half and paint. When dry, glue to the bottom.

More Ideas for your Doll's House

Here are some more fixtures and fittings for your doll's house. The table, chair and staircase are all made out of folded card (cardboard) and the crockery is made out of polymer clay. Make as many chairs, cups and saucers as your dolls will need for themselves and their guests.

YOU WILL NEED
thin coloured card (cardboard)
pencils
craft knife
scissors
crayons
PVA (white) glue and brush
polymer clay
modelling tools
ruler

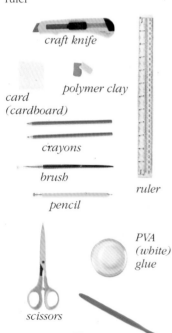

craft knife

card (cardboard)

polymer clay

crayons

brush

ruler

pencil

PVA (white) glue

scissors

modelling tools

1 Trace the furniture shapes from the templates at the front of the book and transfer them on to card (cardboard). Cut out, using a craft knife. Score along the fold lines with scissors.

2 Colour in the shapes with crayons. These are most effective if you build up layers of different colours.

3 Fold the furniture along the fold lines. Check that everything lines up correctly then glue.

4 For the staircase, fold a length of card into a concertina, with flaps on alternate stairs, and glue into place.

5 To make a saucer, flatten a small ball of polmer clay and decorate. Bake as directed on the packet.

6 To make a cup, make a hole in the middle of a small ball of polymer clay and add a small handle.

Fabric Dice

This larger-than-life dice will be useful for many games, and is a great way for children to learn about numbers. If you make two or three dice, they can be used to practise juggling.

YOU WILL NEED
paper
pencil
ruler
assorted fabrics
scissors
sewing thread
needle
stuffing
felt, in assorted colours
fabric glue and brush

fabric

felt

brush

sewing thread

needle

fabric glue

stuffing

scissors

pencil

ruler

1 Make a paper template measuring 12 cm (4¾ in) square. Use to cut out six squares of fabric, in different colours. Allow an extra 6 mm (¼ in) seam allowance all round.

2 With right sides together, stitch two squares along one side, leaving a 6 mm (¼ in) seam. Repeat with the other squares, joining them to make a 'T' shape, as shown.

3 With right sides together, stitch the squares to form a cube, leaving one side open. Turn the cube right side out.

4 Fill the cube with stuffing until it is firm. Stitch the opening.

5 Cut out circles of felt, in different colours for contrast.

6 Glue the felt circles on to the sides of the dice, arranging them as on a real dice.

Character Skittles

Plastic bottles make excellent skittles, especially if you paint them to look like people. You can play the game indoors as well as outside if you use a soft ball.

YOU WILL NEED
clean, empty plastic bottles
fretsaw
newspaper
PVA (white) glue and brush
water
paper baubles
strong glue
acrylic paint, in assorted colours
paintbrush
ribbon, in various colours and
    patterns

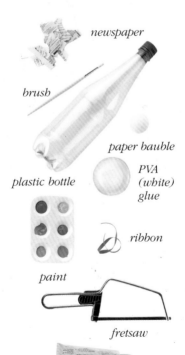

newspaper

brush

paper bauble

plastic bottle

PVA (white) glue

paint

ribbon

fretsaw

strong glue

1 Remove the labels from the bottles by soaking them in water. Saw off the top of each bottle as shown.

2 Cover the bottles in papier-mâché and leave to dry.

3 Glue a paper bauble on top of each bottle, using strong glue.

4 Paint the bottles and the bauble faces with a base coat. Leave the paint to dry.

5 Give each skittle a different character by painting different coloured hair and clothes. Leave the second coat of paint to dry.

6 Tie a piece of ribbon in a bow round the neck of each skittle.

Jumbo Dominoes

This is a giant version of a favourite game, painted in bright colours to make it twice as much fun. Make as many dominoes as you like – a traditional set has 28 pieces, but you will probably only need half that number.

YOU WILL NEED
pine plank wood
ruler
pencil
saw
sandpaper
paint, in assorted colours
paintbrush
sticky black spots
varnish and brush

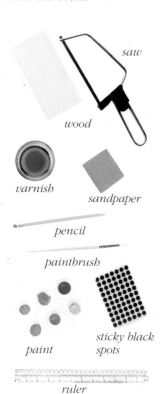

saw

wood

varnish

sandpaper

pencil

paintbrush

paint

sticky black spots

ruler

1 Measure 15 cm x 7.5 cm (6 in x 3 in) rectangles on the wood and cut out. Sand the surfaces and corners thoroughly.

2 Divide each rectangle in half to make two squares. Paint each half a different colour, leaving the paint to dry between each colour.

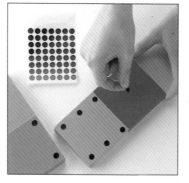

3 Stick black spots on each face of the dominoes. Vary the number of spots from zero to six.

4 Finally varnish the dominoes.

Star Draughts (Checkers)

Make your own painted draughts (checkers) board then make a set of draughts to match. Any small pastry cutter shape would be suitable for the draughts. Play the game the same way as traditional draughts.

YOU WILL NEED
52 cm x 52 cm (20 in x 20 in) MDF (fiberboard)
metal ruler
pencil
emulsion (latex) or acrylic paint, in 2 contrasting colours
paintbrush
masking tape, optional
varnish and brush
polymer clay, in 2 colours to match board
small star pastry cutter

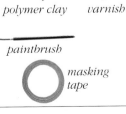

small star pastry cutter

MDF (fiber-board)

pencil

acrylic paint

metal ruler

polymer clay   varnish

paintbrush

masking tape

1 Using a ruler, divide the wood into 64 squares, each measuring 6.5 cm × 6.5 cm (2½ in × 2½ in).

2 Paint alternate squares in the first colour. To help paint straight lines, you can mark out the squares with masking tape and remove it when the paint is dry.

3 Paint the remaining squares with the second colour. When dry, apply a coat of varnish.

4 For the pieces, roll the polymer clay to approximately 5 mm (or ¼ in) thick. Using the pastry cutter, cut out twelve shapes from each colour. Bake, following the manufacturer's instructions, and allow to cool.

Felt Noughts and Crosses (Tic-Tac-Toe)

This game is ideal for train or car trips. The felt shapes are attached to the board with Velcro so they can't move or fall off. Instead of adhesive felt, you can cut out the shapes from ordinary felt squares and stick them on with fabric glue.

YOU WILL NEED
30 cm x 30 cm (12 in x 12 in) thick card (cardboard)
2 squares of adhesive felt, 32 cm x 32 cm (13 in x 13 in) and 30 cm x 30 cm (12 in x 12 in)
adhesive felt, in 3 contrasting colours
pencil
ruler
scissors
thin card (cardboard)
9 Velcro spots
fabric glue and brush

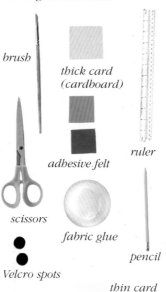

brush

thick card (cardboard)

adhesive felt

ruler

scissors

fabric glue

pencil

Velcro spots

thin card

1 Position the 32 cm (13 in) square of felt centrally on the thick card (cardboard). Stick down, folding the edges over to the back.

2 Stick the 30 cm (12 in) square of felt to cover the back of the card.

3 Cut four narrow strips of contrast-coloured felt 1 cm x 32 cm (¾ in x 13 in). Stick them across the board to make nine equal squares.

4 Trace the templates for the game pieces on to card and cut out. Cover each shape with felt on both sides. You will need four of each shape, using a different colour for the noughts (0s) and the crosses (Xs).

5 Cut out the felt shapes, leaving the card inside.

6 Glue the furry side of the Velcro spots on to the centre of the noughts and crosses. Glue the looped side in the centre of the squares on the board.

Teacup Basketball

This indoor basketball game will certainly cheer up a rainy day. The balls used here are small pompoms available from craft and haberdashery shops. You could also use balls of crumpled paper or table tennis balls.

YOU WILL NEED
pencil
paper
scissors
35 cm x 60 cm (13¾ in x 24 in) card (cardboard)
paint, in assorted colours
paintbrush
bradawl
single-hole punch
thin cord or string
5 coloured pipe-cleaners
electrical tape
pompoms

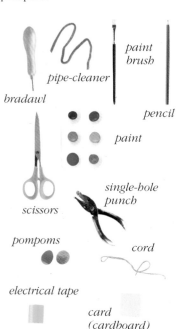

paint brush

pipe-cleaner

bradawl

pencil

paint

single-hole punch

scissors

pompoms

cord

electrical tape

card (cardboard)

1 Trace the teacup template from the front of the book on to paper. Draw round it on to the card (cardboard) five times. Position the shapes as shown.

2 Paint the background, outlining the teacup shapes. When the paint is dry, paint the cups in different patterns. Leave to dry then paint a number (1–5) on each cup.

3 Using a bradawl, pierce a hole on either side of the rim of each cup. Punch a hole in the top corners of the card and thread through cord or string to hang the game on a wall.

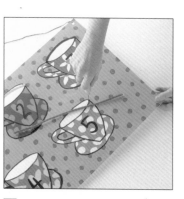

4 Thread a pipe-cleaner through the holes on each cup.

5 On the back of the card (cardboard), coil the ends of the pipe-cleaners and flatten them so they lie flat.

6 Stick pieces of tape over the ends of the pipe-cleaners to secure. Turn the card over and shape the pipe-cleaners so that they stick out in semi-circle basket shapes.

Pyramid Game

This absorbing game will fascinate both children and adults. The object of the game is to move the whole pyramid from one end of the board to the other, moving only one piece at a time and never placing a larger square on a smaller square.

YOU WILL NEED
30 cm x 30 cm (12 in x 12 in)
  of 6 mm (¼ in) birch ply
saw
sandpaper
pencil
drill and 8 mm (⅜ in) bit
15 cm (6 in) of 8 mm (⅜ in)
  diameter dowel
PVA (white) glue and brush
water-based ink, in 5 colours
paintbrush

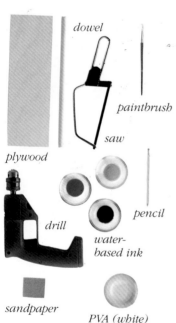

dowel

paintbrush

saw

plywood

drill

pencil

water-based ink

sandpaper

PVA (white) glue

1 Cut a 10 cm (4 in) wide strip from the plywood and sand the edges. Draw a line along the centre then mark points 5 cm (2 in), 15 cm (6 in) and 25 cm (10 in) from one end. Drill holes at these points.

2 Cut the dowel into three equal lengths and sand the ends. Glue into the holes in the plywood.

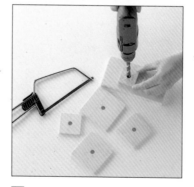

3 Cut squares from the remaining plywood in graduating sizes: 8 cm (3 in), 7 cm (2¾ in), 6 cm (2½ in), 5 cm (2 in) and 4 cm (1½ in). Find the centre of each square and drill a hole.

4 Stain the squares different colours, using water-based ink.

Magnetic Fish

See how many goldfish you can catch – the highest score wins the game. To make a fishing rod, tie a piece of coloured string to the magnet. Tie the other end to a garden stick or cane.

YOU WILL NEED
paper
pencil
thin card (cardboard)
scissors
paint, in assorted colours
paintbrush
coloured metal paperclips
shallow box
magnet

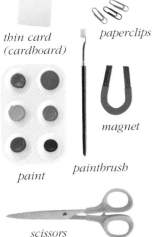

thin card (cardboard)

paperclips

magnet

paint   *paintbrush*

scissors

pencil

1 Trace the fish template on to paper. Draw round the shape five or six times on card (cardboard) and cut out.

2 Paint the fish. Leave to dry then paint a different number on each fish.

3 Attach a paperclip to the mouth of each fish.

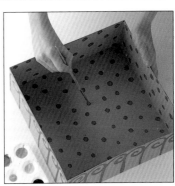

4 Paint the box blue and leave to dry. Using a darker shade, paint wavy lines round the edge to represent water.

Paper Windmill

This pretty windmill spins round in a breeze, but remember it is made of paper so do not leave it outdoors in the rain. Indoors you could use it to decorate one of the toy houses.

YOU WILL NEED
coloured paper, in 3 colours
scissors
PVA (white) glue and brush
ruler
pencil
paperclip
needle, optional
25 cm (10 in) dowel
sandpaper
drill
cork

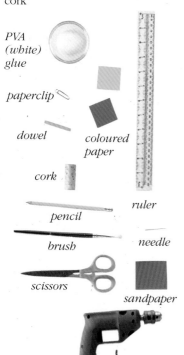

PVA (white) glue

paperclip

dowel

coloured paper

cork

ruler

pencil

brush

needle

scissors

sandpaper

drill

1 Cut out two 15 cm (6 in) squares from paper, each in a different colour. Glue together.

2 Using a pencil, draw a diagonal line across the centre of the square in both directions. Measure 7 cm (2¾ in) from each corner and mark with a dot. Cut up to the dots. Erase the pencil lines.

3 Gently bend every other point into the centre of the square. Glue together, holding the paper in place until the glue hardens.

4 Cut out a small circle from the third colour of paper. Straighten out a paperclip, bend one end into a coil and glue on to the centre of the circle.

5 Gently push the other end of the paperclip through the centre of the windmill, making a hole with a needle first if necessary. Sand the ends of the dowel then drill a small hole 3 cm (1½ in) from one end.

6 Push the sharp end of the paperclip through the dowel. Glue the end of the paperclip and push it into a piece of cork for safety.

Skipping Rope

The simplest toys provide the most fun, and children can play skipping games for hours. Adjust the length of the rope to suit the child's height.

YOU WILL NEED
34 cm (13½ in) coloured plastic tubing
craft knife
sandpaper
approximately 2 m (2¼ yd) smooth coloured rope

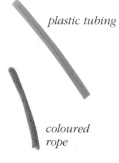

plastic tubing

coloured rope

1 Cut the plastic tubing in half, using a craft knife. Smooth the edges with sandpaper.

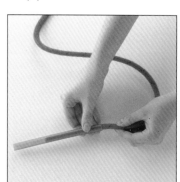

2 Thread each end of the rope through the tube.

craft knife

sandpaper

3 Ask the child to check the length of the rope then knot the ends securely.

4 Burn the ends of the rope to prevent them from fraying.

Mini Pinball

This is a real game of skill and chance. Each player rolls a marble along the tilted board, dodging the players on the field to try and reach one of the goals. The smaller the hole, the higher the score!

You WILL NEED
70 cm x 40 cm (27½ in x 16 in) of 12 mm (⁹⁄₁₆ in) thick MDF (fiberboard)
ruler
pencil
coping saw
sandpaper
1.6 m (1⅔ yd) of 1 cm x 1 cm (½ in x in) wooden lipping
PVA (white) glue
drill
60 cm (24 in) of 8 mm (⁵⁄₁₆ in) diameter dowel
paint, in assorted colours
paintbrush
marbles

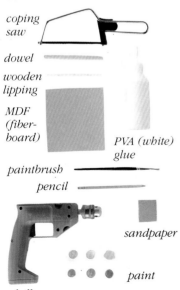

coping saw
dowel
wooden lipping
MDF (fiberboard)
PVA (white) glue
paintbrush
pencil
sandpaper
paint
drill
ruler

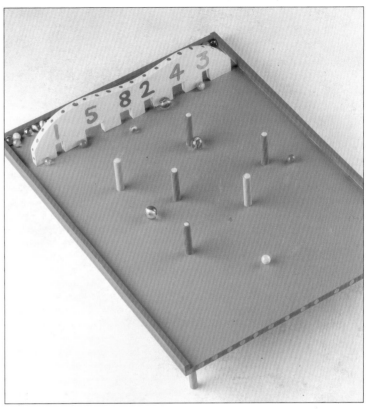

1 Cut a 10 cm (4 in) strip off the short side of the wood. Then cut 5 cm (2 in) off one end. Using a coping saw, cut out holes of different sizes along one long edge. Sand the edges.

2 Cut the lipping into two 60 cm (24 in) strips and one 38 cm (15 in) strip. Glue round the edge of the remaining piece of MDF. Drill six holes at random on one side of the board. On the other side, drill a hole in each corner of one of the short sides.

3 Cut the dowel into eight equal lengths. Glue one into each hole, including the two supports at the back of the board. Glue the other piece of MDF upright near the end of the board, allowing space on either side for the marbles to pass.

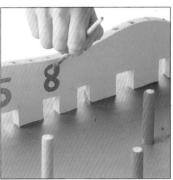

4 Paint the pinball table and leave to dry. Paint score numbers above each hole – the smaller the hole, the bigger the number.

Big Foot Stilts

Children will love walking about on these giant feet! If possible, ask the child for whom the stilts are intended to stand on the cans so that you can measure the length of rope needed.

YOU WILL NEED
2 large, empty cans, the same size
softened plasticine
bradawl
spray paint
enamel paint, in contrasting colour
paintbrush
sticky stars
rope, see above for measurement

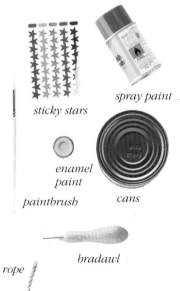

sticky stars

spray paint

enamel paint

paintbrush

cans

rope

bradawl

plasticine

1 Remove the labels from the cans. Place a ball of softened plasticine on either side of the top of each can. Pierce a hole through the plasticine with a bradawl then remove the plasticine.

2 Place the cans on a well-protected surface, preferably outdoors. Spray with spray paint and leave to dry. Spray on a second coat if necessary.

3 Paint the top of the cans with enamel paint. Leave to dry.

4 Decorate the cans with sticky stars.

5 Ask the child to stand on the cans. Measure the length of rope needed then thread one piece of rope through the holes on each can. Tie the ends in a knot.

6 Burn the ends of rope to prevent them from fraying

Soaring Kite

Take this kite out on a windy day and any child will be happy for hours. Choose a bright colour for the tail, to contrast with the kite and show up against the sky.

YOU WILL NEED

50 cm x 70 cm (20 in x 27½ in) lightweight fabric
ruler
pencil
scissors
sewing thread
needle
65 cm (26 in) thin, strong nylon thread
small piece of contrast fabric, for the tail
2 pieces of 5 mm (³⁄₁₆ in) dowel, 68 cm (26¾ in) and 48 cm (19 in) long

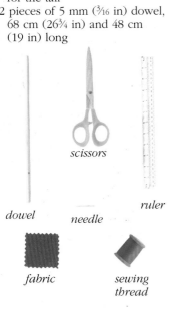

scissors

dowel   *needle*   *ruler*

fabric   *sewing thread*

pencil

1 Fold the fabric in half lengthways. On the raw edges, mark 25 cm (10 in) down from the top. Cut from the fold point at each end to this mark. Open out the kite shape, fold over, place the cut edges together and stitch the seam.

2 Stitch the nylon thread securely to the two corners on either side of the kite.

3 Fold in each corner about 1 cm (½ in). Secure with two tacking stitches about 1 cm (½ in) apart, to go either side of the dowel.

4 Cut a strip of fabric for the tail and stitch on to the bottom of the kite.

5 Lay the two pieces of dowel across the kite and insert the ends into the pockets made by the tacking stitches.

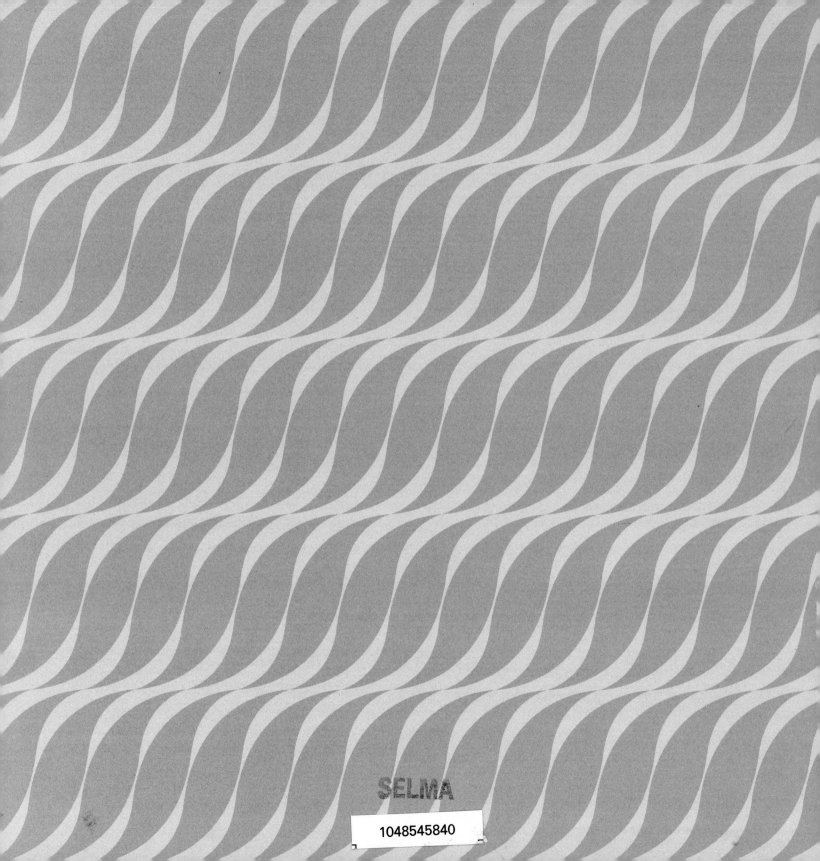

SELMA

1048545840